CAR CRAZY

**LONDON, NEW YORK,
MELBOURNE, MUNICH, AND DELHI**

DORLING KINDERSLEY
Senior Editor Carron Brown
Senior Art Editor Jim Green
Managing Editor Linda Esposito
Managing Art Editor Diane Peyton Jones

Category Publisher Laura Buller
Senior Production Controller Angela Graef
Production Editors Joanna Byrne, Rebekah Parsons-King
DK Picture Library Claire Bowers
Picture Researchers Evi Peroulaki, Liz Moore

Jacket Editor Manisha Majithia
Jacket Designer Mark Cavanagh
Jacket Design Development Manager Sophia MT Turner

Publishing Director Jonathan Metcalf
Associate Publishing Director Liz Wheeler
Art Director Phil Ormerod

DORLING KINDERSLEY INDIA
Designers Niyati Gosain, Neha Sharma
Senior Designer Chhaya Sajwan
Project Designer Shriya Parameswaran
Design Manager Arunesh Talapatra

Editor Sreshtha Bhattacharya
Deputy Editorial Manager Pakshalika Jayaprakash

DTP Designers Arjinder Singh, Jaypal Singh Chauhan,
Saurabh Challariya, Nand Kishor Acharya, Tanveer Zaidi.

DTP Manager Balwant Singh
Production Manager Pankaj Sharma

First published in Great Britain in 2012
by Dorling Kindersley Limited,
80 Strand, London WC2R ORL

A Penguin Company

Copyright © 2012 Dorling Kindersley Limited

2 4 6 8 10 9 7 5 3 1
001 – 182771 – 3/12

A CIP catalogue record for this book is available
from the British Library.

ISBN 978-1-4053-9147-4

Colour reproduction by Media Development & Printing Ltd, UK
Printed and bound in China by Hing Hing

**Discover more at
www.dk.com**

CAR CRAZY

WRITTEN BY
Clive Gifford

CONTENTS

Start the engine

Today, almost a billion cars, trucks, and motorcycles whizz along the world's roads, off-road trails, or on racetracks thrillings thousands of spectators. Motorized vehicles carry people, parcels, food, and much, much more from place to place. In this book, you can read all about the many amazing varieties of cars, trucks, and motorbikes.

TYPES OF CAR

Saloon Family car with four doors and an enclosed boot

Hatchback Smaller car with a sloping rear door and window

Convertible Car with a foldaway or removable roof

Coupé Sporty two-door car that seats 2–4 people

TYPES OF TRUCK

Van High-bodied, small truck for carrying goods

Pickup Light truck with driver's cab and open cargo bed

Flatbed Truck with a large flat cargo bed with no roof or sides

Articulated Truck joined to cargo trailer by a pivot

TYPES OF MOTORBIKE

Cruiser Stylish bike ridden with feet forward of body

Off-road Bike used on tracks, usually with chunky tyres

Scooter Bike with an enclosed engine and small wheels

Sports Fast bike with powerful engine and low riding position

MOTORING FIRSTS

In the 19th century, the very first practical motor vehicles powered by petrol engines were invented.

Designed by Karl Benz in 1885, this three-wheeled **Benz Motorwagen** is thought to be the first motor car.

Built by **Hildebrand and Wolfmüller** in 1894, this first production motorbike had a top speed of 28 mph (45 km/h).

Designed by **Gottlieb Daimler** in 1896, the first truck could carry up to 1,500 kg (3307 lb).

Estate Car with a full-height body all the way to the back

People carrier Minivan that carries six or more people

SUV Four-wheel drive car built on a light truck frame

Limousine Large luxury car, often driven by a chauffeur

Sports High-powered, fast car that may seat just one or two people

Tanker Truck with large tank that holds liquids, such as oil

RV Recreational vehicle or motorhome with living areas

Tourer Long-distance big bike with big engine and fuel tank

WOW!
The speed limit was **4 mph** (6.4 km/h) on English roads in 1896. A man had to walk in front of a car waving a red flag to warn people to move out of the way.

Burning rubber

The lights turn green, the starting flag waves, tyres whirl, and rubber burns into action… the race is on! From long-distance rallies that last weeks to dragster runs that are over in seconds, motor vehicles have been raced ever since they were invented. Top racers need skill, a hunger for speed, and nerves of steel as they drive to the limit. Most of all they need amazing race vehicles with explosive power and incredible performance. Get up to speed on the fastest and most fearsome motorbikes, trucks, and cars around.

Go... karting

Whoosh! Small but speedy, karts are often the first fun on four wheels young racers experience. These low-lying vehicles hug the tracks they race round, and give drivers their first taste of racing, handling turns, and overtaking other vehicles. As drivers become more skilled, they can move to bigger, more powerful karts and superkarts.

CHAMPION ON WHEELS
Formula 1 (F1) legend Michael Schumacher waves to the crowd after a karting race. Like many racing stars, Schumacher began his career in karting and was the European karting champion in 1987 when he was 18 years old.

Rear wheels driven by a chain attached to the engine

HOW TO PETROL ENGINE

1. Fuel and air mixture enters the engine cylinder through inlet valve (top left)

3. Exploding mixture forces the piston down, generating power

2. Inlet valve closes and piston (centre) moves up, squeezing fuel and air mixture

4. Exhaust valve opens and burnt mixture leaves as exhaust gases (top right)

A **Bambino kart** is designed for young racers aged five to eight years, who want to get their first taste of karting.

Superkarts have body panels covering their frames and bigger engines. Some can reach speeds of 155 mph (250 km/h).

FAST FACTS

10 *Karts were invented in the USA in the 1950s. One of the **first engines** in karts was a modified chainsaw motor.*

20 *Karts today are built from a frame of **steel tubes**, which makes the karts strong but light in weight and flexible, too.*

30 ***F1** champs Lewis Hamilton and Sebastian Vettel and **NASCAR** champ Jeff Gordon all began racing in karts.*

Brake pedal helps the kart to slow down

Throttle

Front and side bumpers absorb contact with other karts

WOW!

A superkart can accelerate from 0–60 mph (0–96 km/h) in **under 3 seconds**. It can brake from 100 mph (160 km/h) to zero in around the same time.

RACE TO THE FINISH

A young driver races round a bend on this high-performance Tal-Ko TKM Veloce 4 kart. Powered by fuel from its 8.5-litre (2.25-US gallon) tank, the kart has one foot pedal to brake and one for the throttle, which increases the speed.

ENGINE POWER
17 hp

SPEED
65 mph
(105 km/h)

WEIGHT
83.5 kg
(183.7 lb)

ORIGIN
UK

The Red Bull pit team are busy, busy, busy during an F1 pit stop. They will change the car's four wheels and tyres, and clean the driver's visor in less than six seconds!

HOW TO | F1 CONTROLS

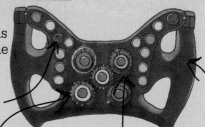

1. Pressing this button puts the driver in radio contact with the race team.

Steering wheel

2. This knob alters the precise mix of fuel injected into the engine.

3. This button boosts engine horsepower for a few seconds on each lap.

FORMULA 1

The crowd roars and tyres squeal as the sleek, high-tech, expensive, and extremely fast F1 cars race around the track. The cars compete in races called Grand Prix and the top 10 finishers gain points to determine who is World Champion. A Grand Prix race lasts about 90 minutes, with cars whizzing round laps of a track. Acceleration and braking are fierce, the driving intense, and speeds reach more than 205 mph (330 km/h) on some tracks.

WOW!
An F1 car's wings create so much downforce that at speeds of more than 150 mph (240 km/h), it could grip the ceiling of a tunnel and be driven **upside down!**

CHAMPION'S F1

The 2010 World Champion Sebastian Vettel races in his Red Bull RB7 car in 2011. At 640 kg (1,411 lb) including the driver, the car is light in weight but fitted with a powerful Renault engine to give it razor-sharp performance.

ENGINE POWER
About 700–800 hp

SPEED
200 mph
(322 km/h)

WEIGHT
640 kg
(1,408 lb)

ORIGIN
Austria/UK

Slick tyres are wide and smooth, designed to grip a dry track really well

FAST FACTS

10 *Many F1 **steering wheels** contain more than 100 working parts and cost more than £20,000 to construct.*

20 *An F1 car can **brake** from its top speed to a standstill in three seconds. Brake discs can heat up to 1,000°C (1,832°F).*

30 *At the end of an F1 race, a car's **tyres** will be so hot (around 120°C or 248°F) that you could cook an egg on them!*

40 ***Michael Schumacher** has won more Grand Prix than any other driver. Of his 91 victories, 13 were won in 2004.*

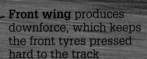

Front wing produces downforce, which keeps the front tyres pressed hard to the track

SPEEDSTERS

Kimi Räikkönen drives his Ferrari F2007 car at the Monza racetrack in Italy. He won the 2007 World Championship.

This **McLaren MP4-23** was the 2008 World Championship winning car. Lewis Hamilton steered it to victory.

Jenson Button races his Brawn BGP 001 round a curve on his way to winning the 2009 World Championship.

A NEED FOR SPEED

The Formula One World Championship began in 1950. Since that time, F1 cars have thrilled millions, but have changed greatly in design. In the past, cars were often built to last many seasons. Today, F1 teams build a new car each year. Modern F1 cars are packed full of electronic aids and safety features. Their top speeds are not much higher than older F1 cars, but their handling, braking, and acceleration means they can complete laps of the track much more quickly.

MASERATI 250F
ORIGIN Italy
YEARS RACED 1954–1958
GRAND PRIX WINS 8
TOP SPEED 180 mph (290 km/h)

FERRARI 312/68
ORIGIN Italy
YEARS RACED 1966–1969
GRAND PRIX WINS 3
TOP SPEED 193 mph (310 km/h)

LOTUS 49
ORIGIN UK
YEARS RACED 1967–1970
GRAND PRIX WINS 6
TOP SPEED 180 mph (290 km/h)

TYRELL P34
ORIGIN UK
YEARS RACED 1976–1977
GRAND PRIX WINS 1
TOP SPEED 186 mph (300 km/h)

LOTUS 79

ORIGIN UK
YEARS RACED 1978–1979
GRAND PRIX WINS 7
TOP SPEED 205 mph (330 km/h)

MCLAREN HONDA MP4/4

ORIGIN UK
YEARS RACED 1988
GRAND PRIX WINS 15
TOP SPEED 210 mph (338 km/h)

FERRARI F300

ORIGIN Italy
YEARS RACED 1998
GRAND PRIX WINS 6
TOP SPEED 210 mph (338 km/h)

MCLAREN-MERCEDES MP4/23

ORIGIN UK and Germany
YEARS RACED 2008
GRAND PRIX WINS 6
TOP SPEED 200 mph (322 km/h)

3. Wheels are turned to point to the right

2. Pinion gear turns clockwise, moving the rack to the left

1. Steering wheel is turned to the right

RACING START

NASCAR stands for the National Association for Stock Car Auto Racing. The NASCAR racing season begins with the Daytona 500 – a 804.7-km (500-mile) race in Florida, USA.

Heavy duty brakes mean drivers can slow sharply at the last moment to enter and leave turns quickly

NASCAR

Meet America's favourite race vehicles – NASCARs. These are souped-up saloons with real brutes of engines, which generate more than five times the power of a regular family car. At least 40 mean machines start a NASCAR race on a track. A lot less finish since NASCAR racing is fast, furious, and really close. This leads to many bumps, bangs, and crashes, with plenty of overtaking and truly amazing racing.

FAST FACTS

10 NASCAR vehicles leave the track to refuel and have all four tyres changed. This **pit stop** often takes less than 15 seconds!

20 More than **60 million people** watched NASCAR events at racetracks and on television in 2010.

30 NASCAR races are long. The longest is the Coca Cola 600, which lasts **400 laps** of a 2.4-km (1.5-mile) track.

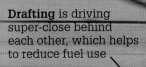
Drafting is driving super-close behind each other, which helps to reduce fuel use

No doors – a driver has to move in and out of the car through the window

Toughened gas tank holds 67.2 litres (17.75 US gallons) of fuel

WOW!
Richard Petty has won **200 NASCAR races**, more than any other driver. He has also finished top 10 in a race a record **712 times!**

ENGINE POWER
850 hp

ORIGIN
USA

WEIGHT
1,542 kg
(3,400 lb)

SPEED
186 mph
(300 km/h)

BUMPER TO BUMPER

NASCAR pickup trucks are equipped with powerful race engines. These reach speeds of around 180 mph (288 km/h).

NASCARs crash during a race. Drivers wear helmets and are protected by a steel tube frame inside the car called a roll cage.

Fast... and faster!

From short sprints to long-distance events that last for days, cars are raced all over the world and in a lot of different ways. Some are raced off-road over bumpy, muddy, or icy ground, but most are raced at great speeds on smooth, fast tracks. Here are four of the most famous races of all.

24 HOURS OF LE MANS
Held in France since 1923, the Le Mans competition sees three drivers per car take turns to keep it travelling on track for 24 hours at a stretch. The car that travels the farthest wins. Here is the 2011 race-winning Audi R18 TDI speeding along during practice.

INDY 500
Indy cars fly into the pits during the 2011 Indy 500. First held in 1911, the Indy 500 is the top race of the IndyCar Series and the USA's most famous motor race. Cars speed round 200 laps of the 4.02-km (2.5-mile) track, nicknamed the Brickyard.

MY STORY:
DAN WHELDON

DATES Born 1978, died 2011
COUNTRY UK
COMPETITION IndyCar Series
INDYCAR SERIES WINS 16
TOP THREE FINISHES 41

Dan Wheldon was only four years old when he first raced in a kart. He came 19th in his first Indy 500 in 2003, but won the race in 2005. In 2011, he won the Indy 500 again, taking the lead on the very last lap. Tragically, he died in a race crash later that year.

MONACO GRAND PRIX

F1 cars whizz around a tight bend as they race through the narrow streets of Monaco. The race was first run in 1929 and features 78 laps of the tough, twisting course, which also includes a tunnel.

DAYTONA 500

Trevor Bayne in car 21 (right) leads in the Daytona 500, the most famous race for NASCARs. Bayne became the race's youngest winner at 20 years and one day old, and also the first driver to win on his very first attempt.

Burnout!

One... two... three... four... five... By the time you count to six, a Top Fuel dragster race is usually over! This is because these mean machines quickly reach speeds of more than 300 mph (480 km/h) as they race head to head along a 402-m (1,319-ft) length of straight track called a drag strip. What's their secret? Massive engines that use an explosive fuel mixture to generate phenomenal power.

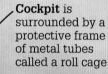

WOW!
In 2005, Tony Schumacher raced a 402-m (1,319-ft) course in under **4.44 seconds** driving a US Army team dragster. That is equal to 336 mph (540 km/h)!

STRAIGHT WINS
The US Army team's Top Fuel dragster races down the track. The driver and engines are positioned close to the rear wheels to help press the tyres down and grip the track. The team's drivers include Tony Schumacher who has won more than 500 dragster races.

Cockpit is surrounded by a protective frame of metal tubes called a roll cage

HOW TO SUPERCHARGER

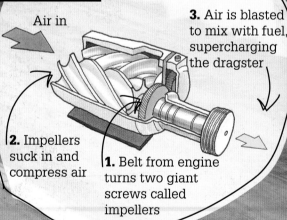

Air in

3. Air is blasted to mix with fuel, supercharging the dragster

2. Impellers suck in and compress air

1. Belt from engine turns two giant screws called impellers

Large wheels are fitted with soft tyres that heat up and grip the track

WHAT A DRAG
Dragsters cross the line at superfast speeds so need a quick way to slow down. Drag chutes are large parachutes that billow out the back of a dragster. These catch air and create the force of drag, slowing the dragster down rapidly.

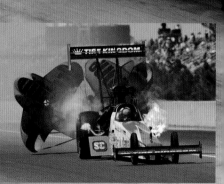

FAST AS LIGHTNING

Powerful drag bikes also race along drag strips. They trail a wheelie bar behind them to stop the bike flipping backwards.

Funny cars look a bit like regular saloon cars, but are lightning fast, reaching speeds of more than 300 mph (480 km/h).

10 *A dragster spins its **rear wheels** on the spot before a race. This leaves rubber on the track to help the wheels grip.*

20 *A quick start is crucial. A Top Fuel dragster can **accelerate** from 0–100 mph (0–160 km/h) in just 0.7 seconds!*

30 *After just 200 m (660 ft) along the racetrack, a dragster can be speeding at **280 mph** (450 km/h).*

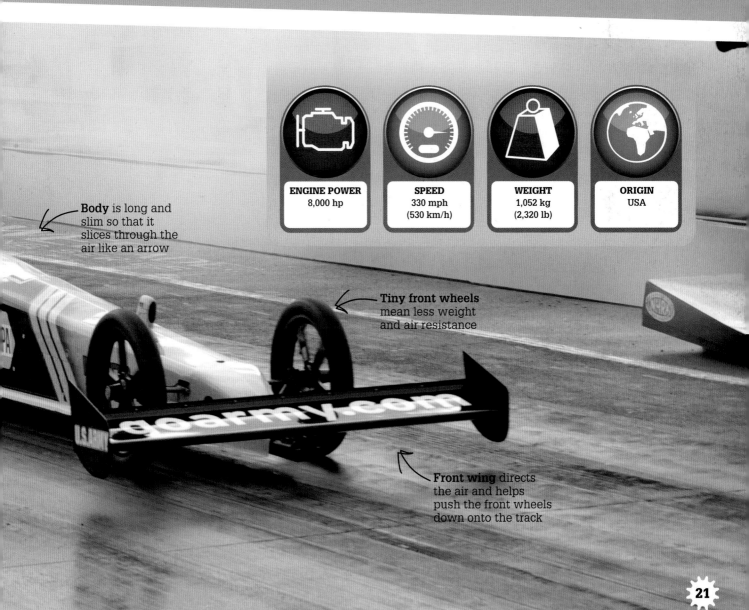

ENGINE POWER	SPEED	WEIGHT	ORIGIN
8,000 hp	330 mph (530 km/h)	1,052 kg (2,320 lb)	USA

Body is long and slim so that it slices through the air like an arrow

Tiny front wheels mean less weight and air resistance

Front wing directs the air and helps push the front wheels down onto the track

Superbikes

Real head-turners, these superbikes are designed for power and speed, whether driven on roads or raced on tracks. Superbikes are top-of-the-range motorcycles fitted with the most advanced brakes and suspension as well as powerful engines. As a result, they are fast, very sensitive to steering, and are suitable only for the most experienced motorcycle riders.

ENGINE POWER
221 hp

SPEED
202 mph plus
(326 km/h plus)

WEIGHT
184 kg
(405.7 lb)

ORIGIN
Italy

FAST FACTS

10 *Honda* and *Ducati* have won 21 out of the first 23 World Superbike Championships since they began in 1988.

20 In 2011, *Jenny Tinmouth* became the first woman to take part in the British Superbike Championship.

30 From a standing start, a superbike can travel 400 m (1,312 ft) in just over *9 seconds!*

Swingarm joins the rear wheel to rest of the superbike, and tilts up and down as part of the suspension

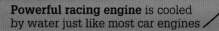

Powerful racing engine is cooled by water just like most car engines

WOW!
The Aprilia RSV4 weighs less than a sixth of a typical family car, but generates **almost twice as much power**.

This **Yoshimura Suzuki GS1000** was used by racer Wes Cooley to win the AMA Superbike Championship in 1979.

Superbikes in the future may be powered by electric motors, such as the sleek racing motorcycle Mission R.

Toughened plastic windscreen makes air flow up and over the rider at high speed

POWER RIDE
Italian racer Max Biaggi leans into a turn on his Aprilia RSV4, as he races round the Phillip Island racetrack in Australia. Riding an RSV4, Biaggi won the 2010 Superbike World Championship.

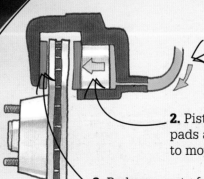

HOW TO DISC BRAKE

1. Brake lever pressed and hydraulic fluid flows down pipe to push piston

2. Piston presses brake pads against disc joined to motorcycle wheel

3. Pads generate force of friction, which slows wheel down

Smooth "slick" tyres for good grip at high speeds

WORLD SUPERBIKE CHAMPIONSHIPS

Leon Haslam leads a trail of riders down into a bend during a World Superbikes race. Two World Superbike races are held each on 13 weekends of the year. Each race is around 100 km (62 miles).

SUPERMOTO

This skilful mix of motocross (see pages 26–27) and road racing uses motocross bikes fitted with road tyres. The bikes are then raced on circuits that are part smooth track and part dirt trail.

MY STORY: BOARD TRACK

LOCATION USA
YEARS 1910–1930s
TOP SPEEDS 100 mph (160 km/h)
LEADING TEAMS Indian, Harley-Davidson, Excelsior

Racing on short, round or oval wooden tracks was hugely popular in the past. The tracks were often steeply angled or banked and took great nerve to race round, especially as racers did not wear helmets and many of the motorbikes used had no brakes.

Revving up!

Motorcycle riders love to race and there are plenty of different competitions to take part in using different types of motorcycle. Many local competitions are held for fun and the challenge, but at the top, motorcycle racers are wealthy and major celebrities. MotoGP star Valentino Rossi, for example, is believed to have earned US$35 million in the 2009 season.

SIDECAR RACING

Sidecars are a wheeled pod fixed to a motorcycle, which holds a passenger. Sleek motorcycle sidecars are raced on tracks. The passenger (below, right) hangs off the sidecar to help the bike keep its balance when cornering.

Casey Stoner powers away during the Doha Grand Prix in 2011

MOTORCYCLE GRAND PRIX

MotoGP motorcycles are handmade specialist racing machines, not available in shops. They are unbelievably fast. At the 2009 Italian Grand Prix, Dani Pedrosa reached a record speed of 217.04 mph (349.29 km/h) on his Honda RC212V.

MADE FOR DIRT

Splat! If you love mud, you will love motocross. Racing takes place round laps of a dirt course complete with dips, tight bends, and hills that send the rider high into the air. With up to 40 competitors starting a single race on such rugged terrain, bumps and crashes are common. Riders need to be strong, skilful, fit, and fearless.

WOW!

Each year, as many as **900 riders** take part in the amazing Enduro du Touquet race in northern France. They race over 16.8 km (10.44 miles) of steep sand dunes.

FAST FACTS

10 Top-level motocross **races** can last around 30–40 minutes and place great strains on a rider's body.

20 Motocross **riders** wear helmets, gloves, and full body protection gear covered with a thin layer of clothing.

30 Dirt bikes are light, agile, and stable, with very **strong suspension** systems to bear heavy landings.

40 In 2004, American motocross legend **Ricky Carmichael** won all 24 out of 24 AMA motocross races.

Chunky tyre tread provides grip when racing through muddy ground

ENGINE POWER
53 hp

SPEED
Around 100 mph
(161 km/h)

WEIGHT
111.9 kg
(246.7 lb)

ORIGIN
Japan

HOW TO | COIL SUSPENSION

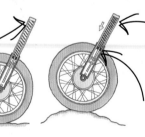

1. Upper mounting fixes to frame of motorcycle

2. Lower mounting fixes to wheel's suspension arm

3. Strong coil spring squeezes up as the vehicle goes over a bump

4. Oil-filled damper reduces the "bounce" caused by spring

MOTOCROSS CHAMPIONSHIPS

Dust clouds rise as 40 riders roar away at the start of the 2007 Oceania Motocross Championships in Australia.

Young motocross riders start their junior race. Motocross is a really popular way for young riders to get into motorsport.

OFF-ROAD BIKE
A quad bike racer becomes airborne during a cross-country race. Quad bikes are off-road vehicles with four wheels, but they have handlebars, which allow riders to steer just like a motorcycle.

Long, curved saddle allows rider to shift body back and forth when jumping

BUMPY LEAP
Built for serious motocross racing, the Yamaha YZ450F has a tough but lightweight aluminium frame and a gutsy engine. There are no lights or licence plate, so the bike cannot travel on roads, but it is built to fly through mud and dirt along off-road tracks.

Footpegs for rider's feet when riding bike on straight parts of the course

27

Get a grip

Once upon a time, off-road vehicles were owned and used only by the military, farmers, and rally racers. Today, millions of people drive four-wheel drive vehicles of varying shapes and sizes. Some are used to carry heavy loads, others assist search and rescue teams in remote areas, but many are used for recreation and exploring country tracks and trails.

CHEVROLET PICKUP
ORIGIN USA
YEAR 1959
LENGTH 529 cm (208 in)
ENGINE 3,859 cc

KAWASAKI BRUTE FORCE 750 ATV
ORIGIN Japan
YEAR 2012
LENGTH 219.5 cm (86.4 in)
ENGINE 749 cc

TATRA T815-7
ORIGIN Czech Republic
YEAR 2004
LENGTH 675 cm (265.7 in)
ENGINE 8,900–10,800 cc

KTM ENDURO 690 R
ORIGIN Austria
YEAR 2009
LENGTH Around 202 cm (80 in)
ENGINE 654 cc

CHEVROLET TAHOE

ORIGIN USA
YEAR 2005
LENGTH 505 cm (198.8 in)
ENGINE 5,300 cc V8

FORD F-150 PICKUP

ORIGIN USA
YEAR 2008
LENGTH 536.4 cm (211.2 in)
ENGINE 4,200 cc V6, 5,400 cc V8

LAND ROVER 90

ORIGIN UK/India
YEAR 2008
LENGTH 389.4 cm (153 in)
ENGINE 2,400 cc

JEEP PATRIOT

ORIGIN USA
YEAR 2007
LENGTH 440.9 cm (173.6 in)
ENGINE 1,968 cc

HOW TO TURBO-DIESEL

1. Powered by a turbine fan, an impeller forces extra air into the engine cylinder.

3. Gases from the explosion leave the engine through the exhaust.

2. The air and diesel fuel mixture is squeezed so much that it gets hot and explodes, creating power.

TRUCK RACING

No, you didn't imagine it. You may be more used to seeing giant tractor cabs powering articulated trucks along roads, but they can also be seen competing against each other on racetracks in front of thousands of fans. Racing is skilful and scarily close. Bumps and scrapes, known as an "exchange of paintwork", often occur as trucks try to overtake and compete for the lead.

WOW!

From a gently rolling start, racing trucks can **accelerate and reach 100 mph** (160 km/h) more quickly than a Porsche 911 sports car!

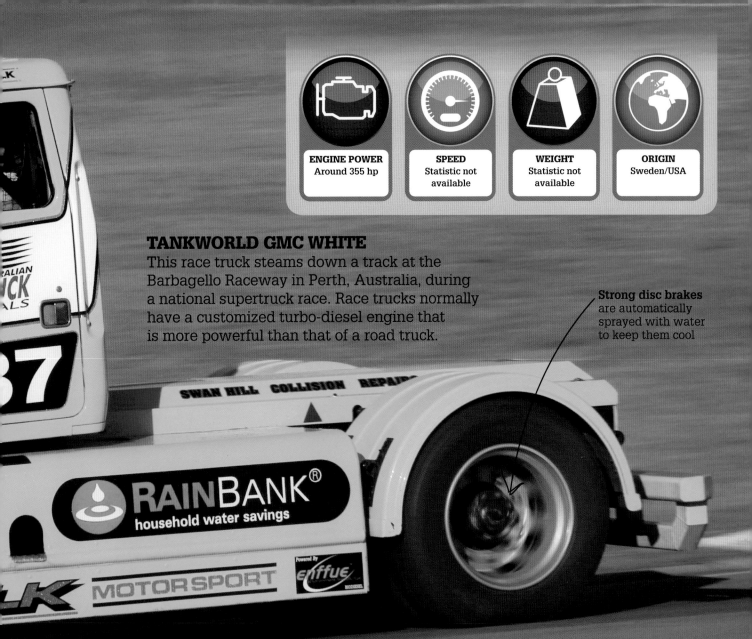

ENGINE POWER	SPEED	WEIGHT	ORIGIN
Around 355 hp	Statistic not available	Statistic not available	Sweden/USA

TANKWORLD GMC WHITE

This race truck steams down a track at the Barbagello Raceway in Perth, Australia, during a national supertruck race. Race trucks normally have a customized turbo-diesel engine that is more powerful than that of a road truck.

Strong disc brakes are automatically sprayed with water to keep them cool

MONSTER WHEELS

School buses, without their usual occupants, battle it out in a race at the Charlotte Motor Speedway track in the USA.

Smoke rises from heavy braking as these trucks speed round the German racetrack called the Nürburgring.

FAST FACTS

10 Truck races last around **8–12 laps** with the speed limited to 100 mph (160 km/h) for safety reasons.

20 At the European Truck Racing Championships, around **120,000 fans** attend a race weekend.

30 The trucks have a **16-gear** gearbox. That is a lot of gear changes to make during a single race.

Thrills and spills

Eat my dust! The ultimate off-road race, the Dakar Rally was first held in 1978. For 30 years, it was run from Paris through Europe and Africa to Dakar in Senegal. In recent years, it has moved to South America. Whatever the continent, the race's punishing course – dusty deserts and rocky terrain – is the toughest of tests. Of the 407 cars, bikes, and trucks that started the 2011 Dakar, only 203 finished.

BEATING THE DUST
Mark Miller's Volkswagen Touareg powers through dusty off-road trails during the 2011 Dakar Rally. Miller and his co-driver, Ralph Pitchford, completed the 5,976-mile- (9,618-km-) long race, finishing sixth. There are three winners of the Dakar Rally, one for each vehicle type – car, truck, and motorbike.

MY STORY:
JUTTA KLEINSCHMIDT

BORN 1962
COUNTRY Germany
FIRST CROSS-COUNTRY RACE
The Pharaoh's Rally of Egypt, 1987
FIRST DAKAR RALLY 1988

Jutta first worked as a BMW car engineer before entering rallies. She was the first woman to complete the 1992 Dakar Rally on a motorcycle. In 2001, driving a Mitsubishi Pajero car, she became the first woman to ever win the Dakar.

CRASHING ON COURSE

A toppled Mitsubishi race vehicle lies in Africa's Sahara Desert during the 1989 Dakar Rally. Sand, mud, heat, rocky plains, and treacherous river crossings test a driver's skill to the limit.

MOTORBIKE RACING

Jean-Christophe Menard revs his motorbike through the dunes of the hostile Atacama Desert in Chile. The all-time leading Dakar motorcyclist is Stéphane Peterhansel with six victories.

TRUCK RACING

A Russian Kamaz truck clambers up a giant sand dune in the Chilean desert during the 2011 race. Trucks are classed in the Dakar Rally as vehicles that weigh more than 3,500 kg (7,716 lb).

Car crushers

Crunch! It's motor-mangling mayhem! In 1981, Bob Chandler performed the first car crush in his Bigfoot 1 vehicle. Not long after, people started calling his creation a monster truck and the name stuck. Today, dozens of these mighty machines, mostly pickup trucks fitted with giant tyres, hefty suspension systems, and big engines, wow spectators at shows.

BLACK STALLION

This monster truck rears up over a collection of crushed cars. Black Stallion has a purpose-built chassis – the frame onto which its body panels and parts are fixed – designed to withstand the impact as it lands after a jump.

FAST FACTS

10 *The monster **tyres** are not fully pumped up so they can squash when driving over objects or landing after a jump.*

20 *In most monster trucks, there are **kill switches** that cut the engine power if a crash or problem occurs.*

30 *Amongst the many Bigfoot vehicles is the **Fastrax**, a former M84 US Army personnel carrier with caterpillar tracks.*

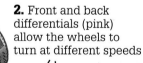

HOW TO FOUR-WHEEL DRIVE

1. Engine powers all four wheels instead of just the front two

2. Front and back differentials (pink) allow the wheels to turn at different speeds

3. When turning a corner, the outer wheel turns faster, so gripping rough or slippery surfaces

WOW!
In 1999,
Bigfoot 14, driven by
Dan Runte, managed a
world record
monster truck jump of
62 m (202 ft) over a
Boeing 727 airliner.

Here's the daddy, the first monster truck, **Bigfoot 1**. It was built in 1979 using a Ford F-250 four-wheel drive pickup truck as a base.

A **Grave Digger** monster truck steams over a row of cars at a show. There have been 27 different Grave Digger trucks built since the first in 1981.

BIGFOOT 5
A woman stands inside the rim of one of Bigfoot 5's wheels. This truly monstrous monster truck weighs more than 12,700.5 kg (28,000 lb). It is fitted with 3.05-m- (10-ft-) tall tyres that were originally used on a US Army road train in Alaska.

ENGINE POWER
1,600 hp

SPEED
Up to 70 mph
(113 km/h)

WEIGHT
4,536 kg
(10,000 lb)

ORIGIN
USA

Daredevils

If you want adrenalin-pumping, non-stop action, then you have come to the right place! Stunt riders and drivers are real daredevils, showing no fear as they perform outrageous leaps, flips, and crashes with trucks, cars, and motorcycles. Some work for movies or perform in front of large crowds. All risk danger and death. Warning: do not try this at home!

LEAP OF FAITH
An Opel stunt car leaps through flames at Walt Disney World's extreme stunt show. The cars in this show are much lighter than regular vehicles and have four reverse gears to help drivers perform their stunts.

CRAZY TRUCKS
It is not every day you can see a full-sized articulated truck pull a wheelie and travel only on its rear wheels! A skilled stunt driver at a Truck Grand Prix event in Germany thrills the crowd with this jaw-dropping move.

LONGEST EVER MOTORCYCLE JUMP

Australian Robbie Maddison breaks the world record for a motorcycle jump in 2008. The daredevil stunt rider leaped 106.98 m (350.98 ft) in one jump!

MY STORY: EVEL KNIEVEL

NAME Robert Craig Knievel
DATES Born 1938, died 2007
COUNTRY USA
CLAIM TO FAME Ultimate Motorcycle Daredevil

Knievel became a worldwide star in the 1970s by attempting stunts others only dared to dream about. Sometimes he failed, breaking 433 bones during his career. Ouch! One triumphant stunt saw him leaping 14 buses in Ohio, USA. His son, Robbie, also a stunt motorcyclist, jumped the Grand Canyon in 1999.

CAR STUNT DISPLAYS

A Hollywood movie stunt team called Filmka performs in front of crowds in Taizhou, China, balancing carefully on a moving car. The car's driver has tilted the car so that it travels along on only two wheels on one side.

FREESTYLE MOTOCROSS

This rider performs a daring stunt called a superman seat grab. He lets go of his Honda dirt bike, then holds on to the seat with just one hand! Freestyle motocross (FMX) competition judges mark riders on the quality of jumps.

HARLEY FAT BOY

When childhood friends William Harley and Arthur Davidson built their first "motorized bicycle" in 1903, they had no idea what they had begun. By 1920, Harley-Davidson was the world's biggest motorcycle maker. The company has had its ups and downs since, but today is world famous for its heavyweight bikes that are used for touring long distances or cruising city streets in style.

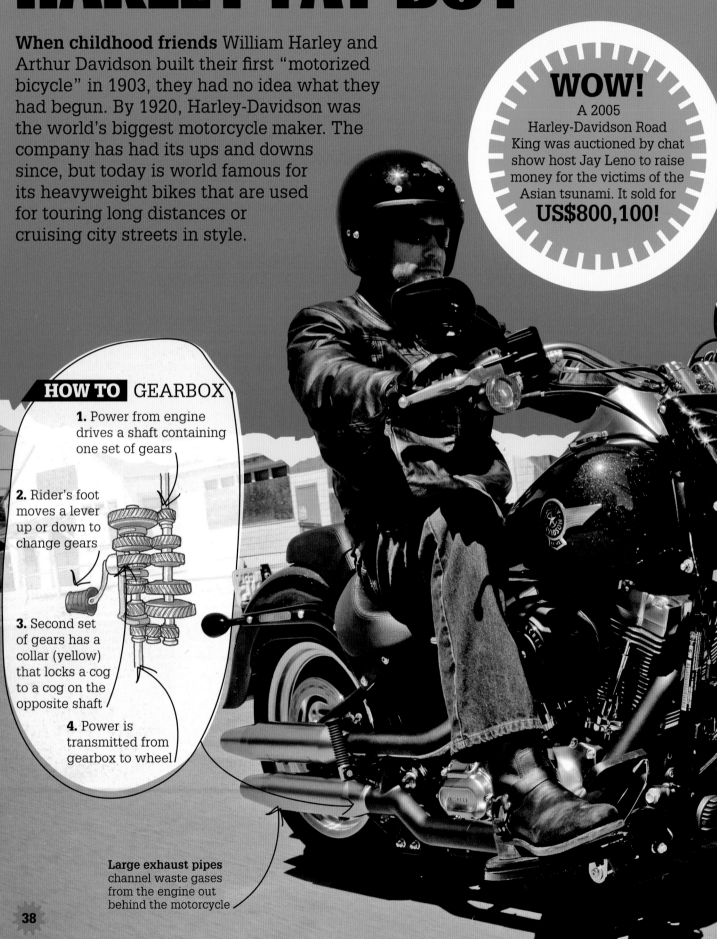

WOW!
A 2005 Harley-Davidson Road King was auctioned by chat show host Jay Leno to raise money for the victims of the Asian tsunami. It sold for **US$800,100!**

HOW TO GEARBOX

1. Power from engine drives a shaft containing one set of gears

2. Rider's foot moves a lever up or down to change gears

3. Second set of gears has a collar (yellow) that locks a cog to a cog on the opposite shaft

4. Power is transmitted from gearbox to wheel

Large exhaust pipes channel waste gases from the engine out behind the motorcycle

(10) The first Harley-Davidsons were driven by a **leather belt**. They had to be pedalled like a bike to start the engine.

(20) Harley-Davidsons have appeared in many **movies**, such as The Wild One and Terminator 2.

(30) More than 3,400 **police** departments ride Harley-Davidsons in the USA alone.

This **classic chopper** style Harley has long handlebars and its fuel tank is painted with the American flag.

With a windscreen and rear storage room, the **Electra Glide** is a big touring motorcycle for long-distance journeys.

2012 FAT BOY

With a large, comfortable bucket seat and a 200 mm-wide fat rear tyre, the Fat Boy is a motorbike for laid-back riding. But its hefty air-cooled engine and six-speed gearbox mean it can pull away sharply when needed.

Long front forks allow the wheel plenty of room to move up when it hits rough ground

Mudguard protects rider from spray and mud thrown up by 140-mm- (5.5-in-) wide front tyre

ENGINE POWER
1,584 cc

SPEED
112 mph
(180 km/h)

WEIGHT
315 kg
(694 lb)

ORIGIN
USA

PROUD OWNERS

Harley-Davidson motorbikes cruise in convoy down a city street. Harley owners are very loyal and enthusiastic about their machines. The Harley Owners Group (HOG) has more than one million members.

FAST WHEELS

Blink… and you will miss it. For those people with a lot of money and a need for sensational speed and style, supercars offer the ultimate in performance. Built in small numbers with great attention to detail, they cannot carry all of your shopping, but they will burn serious rubber. Filled with the latest technology, a supercar's low profile helps it slice through the air at high speed.

WOW!
In 2010,
a Veyron reached
267.9 mph
(431.07 km/h) in a test run.
That is equal to 119 m
(390 ft) every second!

Advanced brakes can slow down the car from 249–0 mph (400–0 km/h) in under 10 seconds

FAST FACTS

10 The Veyron is named after **Pierre Veyron**, the racing driver who won the 1939 Le Mans 24 Hour (see page 18).

20 Heat from the giant engine and fast speeds is an issue so the Veyron has a staggering **10 radiators**.

30 Driving at the Veyron's **top speed**, the car's 100-litre (26.4-US gallon) tank would empty around 80 km (50 miles).

BUGATTI VEYRON
This snarling beast of a machine was the world's fastest production car when it was launched in 2005. Propelled by an enormous 16-cylinder engine, it can zoom from 0–124 mph (0–200 km/h) in just 7.3 seconds. That is FAST!

HOW TO AERODYNAMICS

2. The Veyron's streamlined shape helps air to flow smoothly over the surface. This reduces air resistance.

3. The rear wing, called a spoiler, creates a downward force to help keep the car on the road at high speeds.

1. A car is slowed by resistance from the air it drives through, especially at high speeds.

Car body lowers to help grip the ground at high speeds

BUGATTI

This powerful Italian supercar, the **Pagani Zonda**, has a lightning-fast top speed of 220 mph (354 km/h).

The sleek **Lamborghini Diablo** can race to 62 mph (100 km/h) in about 4.5 seconds and reach a speed of 202 mph (325 km/h).

ENGINE POWER
1,050 hp

SPEED
268 mph
(431 km/h)

WEIGHT
1,888 kg
(4,162 lb)

ORIGIN
France/Germany

41

Supercars

Supercars are limited edition, high-performance sports cars with a twist. Buy one and you will well and truly stand out from the crowd. That is if they can see you as you race by in a blur. All of the amazing supercars featured on these pages are lightning fast from a standstill, packed with high-tech engine technology, and have top speeds of more than 200 mph (322 km/h).

MERCEDES-BENZ SL65

ORIGIN Germany
BUILT 2005
ENGINE POWER 604 hp
TOP SPEED 200 mph (322 km/h)

BENTLEY CONTINENTAL SUPERSPORTS

ORIGIN Germany
BUILT 2009
ENGINE POWER 620 hp
TOP SPEED 204 mph (328 km/h)

FERRARI 599 GTB

ORIGIN Italy
BUILT 2009
ENGINE POWER 612 hp
TOP SPEED 205 mph (330 km/h)

LAMBORGHINI MURCIÉLAGO 670

ORIGIN Italy
BUILT 2009
ENGINE POWER 670 hp
TOP SPEED 213 mph (343 km/h)

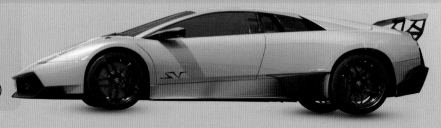

In 2009, the Bertone Mantide was unveiled, with a light carbon-fibre body, streamlined shape, and a speed of 217 mph (351 km/h). Bertone also designed the Stratos Zero and the Alfa Romeo BAT 9 (see page 50).

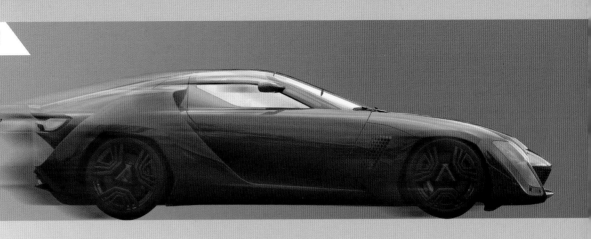

ASTON MARTIN ONE-77

ORIGIN UK
BUILT 2011
ENGINE POWER 750 hp
TOP SPEED 220 mph (354 km/h)

RUF PORSCHE CTR3

ORIGIN Germany
BUILT 2007
ENGINE POWER 691 hp
TOP SPEED 233 mph (375 km/h)

SHELBY SSC ULTIMATE AERO TT

ORIGIN USA
BUILT 2007
ENGINE POWER 1,183 hp
TOP SPEED 257 mph (413 km/h)

KOENIGSEGG CCX-R

ORIGIN Sweden
BUILT 2006
ENGINE POWER 1,064 hp
TOP SPEED 250 mph (402 km/h)

Supersonic!

Meet the record-breakers! Plenty of cars, trucks, and motorbikes seem really fast. Here, though, are the real deals — the fastest land vehicles on the planet. These record-breaking speedsters take many years to design and test. Many use aircraft engines and even rockets to propel them forward, usually across giant salt flats that offer a super smooth surface to race on.

THRUST SSC
Holder of the title "the fastest car on Earth" since 1997, Thrust SSC was powered by two military jet engines. A jet pilot, Wing Commander Andy Green, steered it to reach its record speed of 763.04 mph (1,227.96 km/h).

MY STORY: BLOODHOUND SSC

AIM To break the 1,000 mph (1,600 km/h) barrier
COUNTRY UK
DRIVER Andy Green

Under development, the Bloodhound SSC features two engines. A jet engine usually found in a Eurofighter aircraft will accelerate the car to more than 350 mph (563 km/h) in just 15 seconds. Then, a rocket engine ignites to blast Bloodhound towards, and hopefully past, the 1,000 mph (1,609 km/h) barrier. Wow!

FASTEST DIESEL-POWERED VEHICLE

The JCB444 engine powers tractors and diggers. In 2006, though, a pair of these engines propelled the JCB Dieselmax to 328.767 mph (529 km/h), breaking the old world record by almost 93 mph (150 km/h)!

FASTEST MOTORCYCLE

The Top Oil Ack-Attack is a motorcycle covered with a smooth, sleek body specially designed so it can cut through the air. In 2010, it reached a record speed of 376.2 mph (601.85 km/h).

FASTEST WHEEL-POWERED CAR

Some record-breakers do not power their wheels, but use thrust from the engines to move. Spirit of Rett is the fastest car using a single engine to drive its wheels round… and fast! In 2010, it sped to 414.32 mph (666.8 km/h).

Dream wheels

Gleaming chrome, exciting paint jobs, powerful engines, and outrageous bodywork. It is no surprise that so many people dream of owning the coolest motorbikes and hottest cars around. Welcome to the world's sportiest supercars, luxury limos, big bikes, and crazy cars that think they are aircraft or boats. We also meet the pioneering vehicles that gave millions of people their first chance to go car crazy.

FORD MODEL T

Meet the historic car that changed motoring forever.
In 1908, Henry Ford's Model T first rolled off the
production line. Sturdy, reliable, and with standard spare
parts, it was a fraction of the cost of rival cars and it
revolutionized motoring. Nicknamed the Tin Lizzy,
the Ford Model T was the first car that millions
of people in the USA could afford to buy.

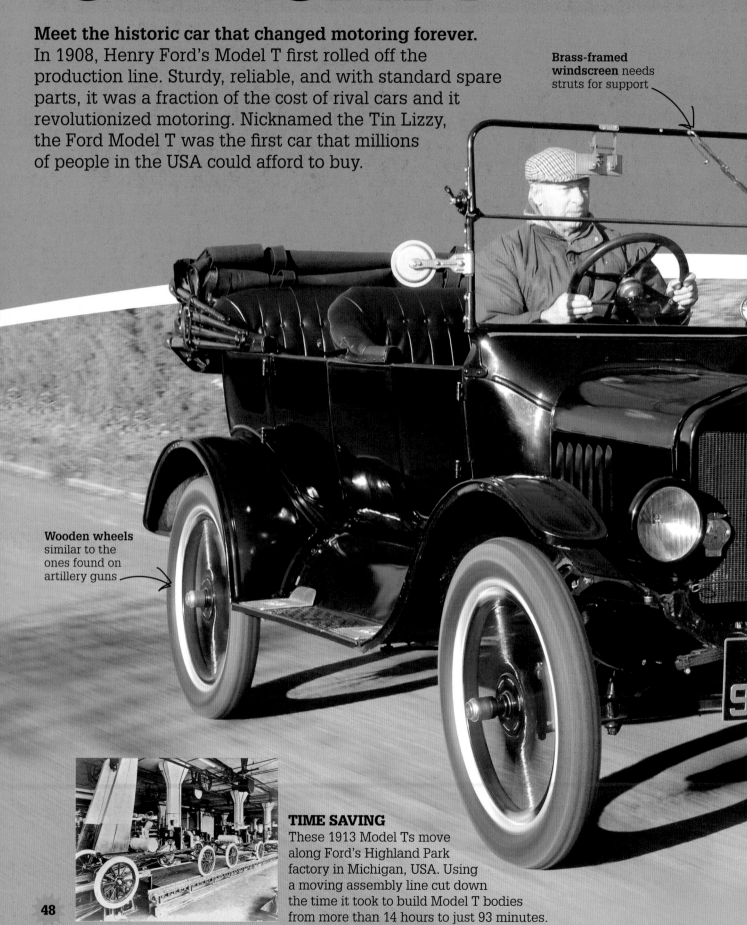

**Brass-framed
windscreen** needs
struts for support

Wooden wheels
similar to the
ones found on
artillery guns

TIME SAVING
These 1913 Model Ts move
along Ford's Highland Park
factory in Michigan, USA. Using
a moving assembly line cut down
the time it took to build Model T bodies
from more than 14 hours to just 93 minutes.

DIFFERENT STYLES

Many different versions of Model T Fords were made. This **1915 Roadster** had a short body and a soft-top roof.

This classic **1924 Model T Ford Speedster** features a racy boat-tail body design that tapers from the seats towards the rear wheels.

ENGINE POWER
22 hp

SPEED
30–35 mph
(48–56 km/h)

WEIGHT
540 kg
(1,200 lb)

ORIGIN
USA

WOW!
More than
15 million
Ford Model Ts were made from 1908 until 1927, the most of any single type of car until the Volkswagen Beetle.

FAST FACTS

10 *The first Model Ts had only one dial on the* **dashboard**, *which showed the battery's electric current.*

20 *From 1914 to 1926, all Model Ts were* **painted black**. *Before then, some were blue, red, green, or grey.*

30 **Sales** *were so strong that by 1918, half of all cars in the USA were Ford Model Ts.*

40 *Only* **11 Model Ts** *were built in its first month of production. In 1923, more than two million cars were built.*

HOW TO ACETYLENE-POWERED LIGHTS

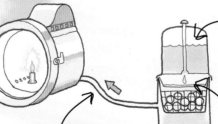

1. Upper container full of water and bottom full of calcium carbide chips

2. Driver presses valve that drips water onto the chips, creating acetylene gas

3. Gas travels along pipe to headlights where it burns to provide light

CRANK IT UP
This 1910 Model T Ford was started by turning a crank handle at the front of the engine. The car had just two forward gears and used gas lamps rather than electric lights.

CONCEPT CARS

Check out these crazy vehicles. Have the designers gone nuts? Far from it. Concept cars are built by companies to try out new technology and features or to showcase cutting-edge vehicle shapes, styles, and designs. Behind the funny, sometimes outrageous, looks is often important technology, which ends up in more ordinary-looking production cars a few years later.

Y-JOB
MAKER Buick Automobiles
DATE BUILT 1938
FEATURES Electric doors, power-operated convertible roof

BAT 9
MAKER Alfa Romeo
DATE BUILT 1955
FEATURES Sleek design, large tail fins, highly streamlined

FIREBIRD III
MAKER General Motors
DATE BUILT 1958
FEATURES Twin bubble cockpits, air brakes, joystick steering

STRATOS ZERO
MAKER Bertone and Lancia
DATE BUILT 1970
FEATURES 84 cm (33 in) tall, fibreglass body, windscreen door

The Chevrolet Super Sports Roadster (SSR) proved that looks are not everything. As a concept in 2003, it had promise – a two-seat pickup truck with a convertible roof. However, the mechanics were not strong. Few trucks were sold and production shut in 2006.

F 300 LIFE-JET
MAKER Mercedes-Benz
DATE BUILT 1997
FEATURES Three wheels, tilt control, foldable roof sections

KAZ
MAKER IDEA Institute
DATE BUILT 2001
FEATURES Stretch limo, eight electrically powered wheels

PIVO 2
MAKER Nissan
DATE BUILT 2007
FEATURES Wheels rotate to drive in any direction

LIFECAR
MAKER Morgan
DATE BUILT 2008
FEATURES Electronic gears, fuel cells power electric engine

THE BEETLE

In the 1930s, the German government called for a "people's car" that most families could afford. The result was the Volkswagen Beetle. Small and simple yet packed full of clever advances such as in-car heating and an air-cooled engine, it caused a sensation. Since then, Beetles have stretched into limousines, run on sand as dune buggies, raced in rallies, and been fitted with sirens as police cars.

Under the front bonnet lies luggage space and spare tyre

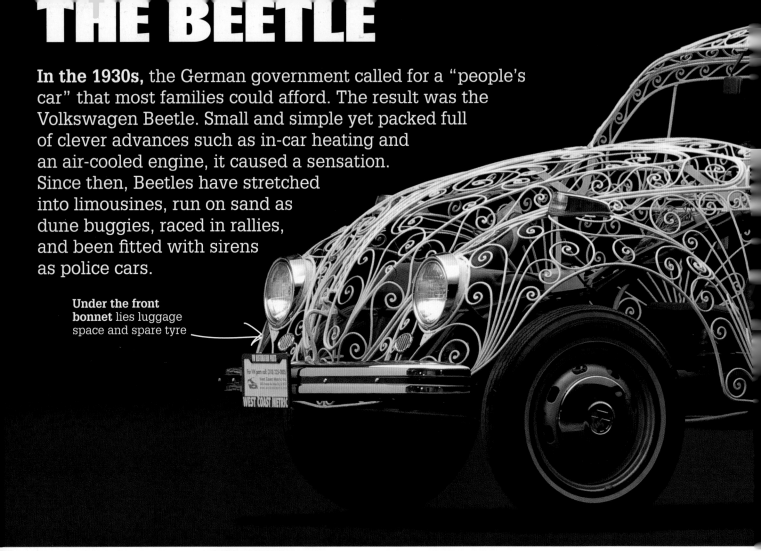

EARLY BEETLES
The body shells of some 1960 Beetles hang from a production line in Germany. Throughout its long life, more than 70,000 different changes and improvements were made to the car's design.

BAJA BUG
Many Beetles were modified to run off-road. These were called Baja Bugs. This 1969 Baja Bug, called Pedro, made a charity run from the UK to Australia, a distance of more than 31,000 km (19,263 miles).

BIRDCAGE BEETLE

The body of this astonishing Beetle is made out of wrought ironwork, such as you might find on a garden gate or old birdcage. It is displayed in Volkswagen's museum in Wolfsburg, Germany.

Rear passenger window swings out to the side to let in air

Compact engine packed into the rear of the car body

BEETLE RALLY

More than a thousand VW Beetles parade through the German city of Berlin before the premiere of the movie *Herbie Fully Loaded* about a Beetle with a mind of its own.

MY STORY: MILESTONE BEETLE

LOCATION Germany
DATE 1955
MILESTONE One millionth Volkswagen car
WHERE ZeitHaus Museum, Autostadt, Wolfsburg

To celebrate their one millionth car, Volkswagen painted it gold and covered its front bumper in rhinestones. It was the first of many milestones. By the time production of Beetles stopped in 2003, a staggering 21,529,464 cars had been built.

ALUMA COUPÉ

ORIGINAL MAKE OF CAR
Built from scratch
YEAR OF ORIGIN 1991
FEATURE Powerful engine

FLAMING FORD

ORIGINAL MAKE OF CAR
Ford Hi Boy Coupé
YEAR OF ORIGIN 1932
FEATURE Painted flames

SOUPED-UP COUPÉ

ORIGINAL MAKE OF CAR
Willys Americar Coupé
YEAR OF ORIGIN 1941
FEATURE 750 hp engine

BRILLIANT BEL AIR

ORIGINAL MAKE OF CAR
Chevrolet Bel Air
YEAR OF ORIGIN 1952
FEATURE Enclosed rear wheels

HOT RODS

Vrmmm, vrmmm! Welcome to the world of the wild, wacky, and wonderful hot rods. These cars were a big hit in California, USA, in the 1950s, when old Model T and Ford coupé cars from the 1920s and 1930s were fitted with big engines and often given highly colourful paint jobs. With fewer old cars available to work on today, many hot rod makers are turning to other makes of vehicle to customize or even building one-off cars from scratch.

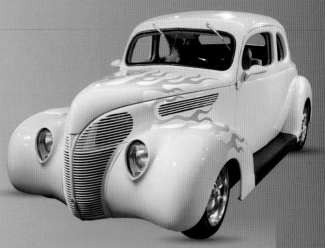

LOW LIGHTING
ORIGINAL MAKE OF CAR
Ford Coupé
YEAR OF ORIGIN 1934
FEATURE Low-slung lights

ALL UP FRONT
ORIGINAL MAKE OF CAR
Ford Coupé
YEAR OF ORIGIN 1938
FEATURE Top-mounted wipers

CHEVY CHEZOOM
ORIGINAL MAKE OF CAR
Chevrolet Bel Air
YEAR OF ORIGIN 1957
FEATURE Sports car suspension

THE DETONATOR
ORIGINAL MAKE OF CAR
BMW Isetta 600 microcar
YEAR OF ORIGIN 1958
FEATURE Powerful V8 engine

HAT'S AMAZING!

Hot rods became iconic symbols in 1983 after a 1930s Ford, like this one (right), featured on the cover of rock band ZZ Top's album Eliminator. Originally racing cars, today's hot rods are often made for display.

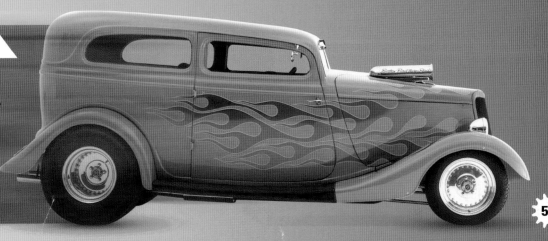

Raw power

Built for speed, this outrageous motorbike is not even allowed on the roads, only on private land. Concept motorbikes such as this are built singularly or in very small numbers. They allow designers to test out all sorts of ideas about how motorbikes in the future might look. Sometimes, a handful of exciting concept motorbikes go on sale. The Dodge Tomahawk is one of the lucky few to hit the showroom floor.

WOW!
No longer for sale, it is believed that only nine Dodge Tomahawks were ever sold. You needed a huge wallet to buy one. Each bike cost around **US$555,000!**

FAST FACTS

10 The Dodge Tomahawk was introduced at the *2003* North American International Auto Show.

20 The seat and body panels are sculpted from a single giant **680 kg** (1,500 lb) block of aluminium.

30 The bike's **suspension** means a rider can lean sharply into a turn, but keep all four wheels on the ground.

40 The powerful **Viper engine** can propel the Tomahawk from 0–60 mph (0–96 km/h) in 2.5 seconds.

FOUR WHEELER
The Dodge Tomahawk is really a quad bike design, as it has two front and two rear wheels. These are powered by an absolute beast of an engine normally given in a Dodge Viper sportscar. As a result, the motorbike is a true super fast driver.

Front disc brake

Row of 22 bright LED headlights sandwiched between two front wheels

ENGINE POWER
500 hp

SPEED
300 mph
(480 km/h)

WEIGHT
680.4 kg
(1,500 lb)

ORIGIN
USA

MOTORBIKES OF THE FUTURE

The **Honda T2** concept bike features giant chrome exhausts and a large blue mudguard over the rear wheel.

Unveiled in 2007, the **Suzuki Biplane** is a bright yellow beast with a 1,000 cc engine and a low riding position.

This aluminium-framed **Victory Core** motorbike lets it all hang out with the engine and suspension on show.

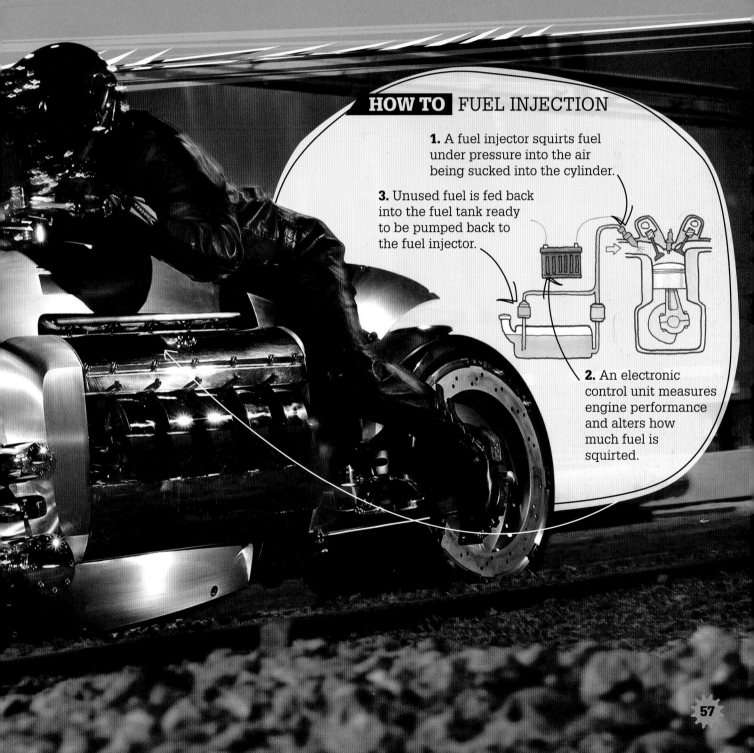

HOW TO FUEL INJECTION

1. A fuel injector squirts fuel under pressure into the air being sucked into the cylinder.

3. Unused fuel is fed back into the fuel tank ready to be pumped back to the fuel injector.

2. An electronic control unit measures engine performance and alters how much fuel is squirted.

Take a stretch

Smooth! From electric tinted windows to DVD players, bars, and fridges, stretch limousines or limos are the last word in luxury transport. Stretch limos are built by companies called coachbuilders. They cut a luxury car in two just behind the front seats. They then add extra lengths of body in the middle. Some longer limos require extra sets of wheels for support.

Tinted windows allow driver and passengers to see out, but stops people on the outside looking in

FAST FACTS

10 When a car is stretched, it becomes **heavier**. Heavier cars are harder to stop so limos have more powerful brakes.

20 Due to their length, many limos have reversing **cameras** that project the view behind the car onto a screen.

30 Midnight Rider is an articulated truck that has been turned into a luxury **limo restaurant** seating 40 people.

LUXURY LIMOS

Stretch limousines such as this pink **Lincoln** can be brightly coloured and are normally driven by a chauffeur.

This giant eight-wheeled **stretch Hummer** limo can hold up to 16 passengers. This huge limo even has a dance floor that lights up.

STYLE ON WHEELS

This Mini XXL is one of a kind, created by adding extra sections to the middle of the car's body. Not only can it seat six people, but pull off the cover at the back and there is a hot tub!

WOW!

A stretch limo built by Jay Ohrberg is the biggest in the world with **26 wheels**, a swimming pool, king-size bed, and helipad for landing helicopters on.

GLAMOROUS INSIDE

Kick back and enjoy. The interior of a limousine is often fitted out with a bar, air conditioning, groovy lighting, and a thumping surround sound music system. The cars are often hired for special occasions, such as weddings and birthdays.

ENGINE POWER
200 hp

SPEED
141 mph
(226 km/h)

WEIGHT
Statistic not
available

ORIGIN
USA

HOW TO AIR CONDITIONING

4. Cooled air is blown into the vehicle

1. Compressor squeezes the refrigerant gas moving through pipes

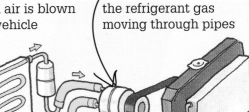

3. Circulating through low-pressure tubes, refrigerant expands and becomes much colder

2. Gas becomes liquid in condensor and becomes very warm

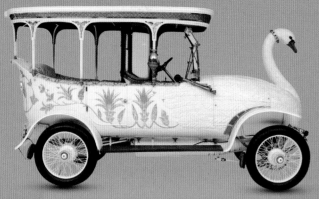

BROOKE 25/30 HP SWAN

ORIGIN UK
BUILT 1910
FEATURES Swan head sprayed water to clear the road of people

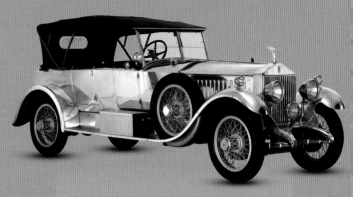

ROLLS ROYCE PHANTOM I

ORIGIN UK
BUILT 1925
FEATURES Handmade leather seats, foldaway roof

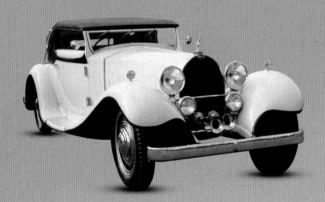

BUGATTI TYPE 41 ROYALE

ORIGIN France
BUILT 1933
FEATURES 12,700 cc engine, whalebone dashboard knobs

CADILLAC FLEETWOOD BOUGHAM

ORIGIN USA
BUILT 1965
FEATURES Electric windows, wooden panelled interior

LUXURY CARS

Welcome to the cars that say prestige and power. Ever since motor cars were invented, some people paid more to own the very best vehicles. Luxury cars tend to be larger and more spacious than regular cars, and are packed full of creature comforts and entertainment features. Many modern luxury cars are brilliant to drive, but owners often employ chauffeurs to do the driving for them.

MERCEDES-BENZ 560

ORIGIN Germany
BUILT 1985
FEATURES Anti-lock braking,
1988 version had heated seats

JAGUAR XJ12

ORIGIN UK
BUILT 1972–1997
FEATURES Power steering,
leather seats, air conditioning

AUDI A5 COUPÉ

ORIGIN Germany
BUILT 2007
FEATURES Hi-fi system with
14 speakers, multimedia screen

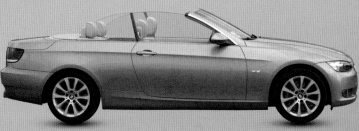

BMW 3-SERIES CONVERTIBLE

ORIGIN Germany
BUILT 2009
FEATURES Electric foldaway
roof, in-car Internet

THAT'S AMAZING!

Even though the Rolls Royce Phantom Drophead weighs almost 2,722 kg (6,000 lb), it has a top speed of 155 mph (249 km/h), and can accelerate from 0–60 mph (0–96 km/h) in just 5.6 seconds.

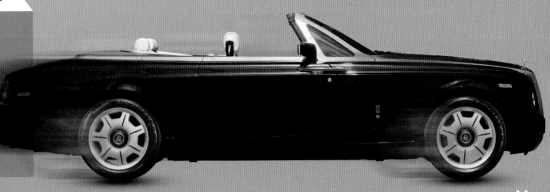

BIG VS SMALL

From giant earth-movers to tiny city rides, size matters in the world of wheels. Some of the biggest trucks are used in the mining industry whilst the largest motorbikes are built for fun. At the other end of the scale are miniscule bikes and cars – 90 Peel P50 cars weigh about the same as one mining truck tyre!

PEEL P50

Meet the smallest production car ever! The single seater Peel P50 cost just £199 when it went on sale in 1963. The tiny vehicle had no reverse gear, but that was not a problem. You simply got out of the car, picked it up, and turned it round yourself!

MINIMOTO

Minimoto motorcycles are tiny, tiny, tiny – less than 50 cm (20 in) tall and under 1 m (39 in) long. Their small engines produce only 4–6 hp, but because they are so small and light, they can race along karting circuits at high speeds.

DREAM BIG

The world's tallest motorbike stands 3.429 m (135 in) high. Its tyres alone are 1.88 m (6.2 ft) tall. It has seats for a driver and five passengers. Those handlebars are just for show, though. Dream Big is steered using a steering wheel.

MONSTER EARTH-HAULER

This Caterpillar 797B truck is a giant earth mover used in construction and mining. Its massive 106,000 cc engine has 20 separate cylinders and uses 8 litres (2 US gallons) of fuel for every kilometre (0.62 miles) travelled. At 6.5 m (21 ft 6 in) high, this truck dwarfs its driver.

MY STORY: LIEBHERR T282B

ORIGIN Germany, 2004
JOB Dumper truck
ENGINE POWER 3,650 hp
FUEL TANK 4,732 litres (1,250 US gallons)

This gigantic truck can carry up to 372 tonnes (360 US tons) of earth and rock at a speed of up to 40 mph (64 km/h). The truck is so heavy that it is not allowed on public roads as it would completely crush the tarmac surface.

Six tyres – each weighs 5,300 kg (11,680 lb)

JET POWER

The Aquada's V6 petrol engine drives its wheels on the road and powers a large jet thruster when afloat. The jet sucks in water and squirts it out the back with great force, generating almost 1,000 kg (2,205 lb) of thrust.

ENGINE POWER	SPEED	WEIGHT	ORIGIN
175 hp	Water: 35 mph (56 km/h); land: 100 mph (161 km/h)	1,750 kg (3,858 lb)	UK and USA

Gibbs Aquada

Vroom! Splash! Is it a car or a boat? It's both! This amazing amphibious vehicle can travel on land and water. The 4.81-m- (15.8-ft-) long Aquada is the brainchild of New Zealander Alan Gibbs. In the blink of an eye, it transforms from a sporty three-seater car to a speedy motor boat – just add water! Amphibious vehicles must be able to float without leaking, and be powered to move well on roads and seas.

FAST FACTS

(10) *Be prepared to raid the piggy bank if you fancy one of these cars. They cost around £150,000 ($295,110)!*

(20) *The Aquada has **no doors**, which helps to stop leaks. Each part has had a salt-spray test that lasts 2,000 hours.*

(30) *Gibbs Technologies recently unveiled the first **Quadski** – a quad bike that turns into a jet ski in seconds!*

(40) *The 67-litre (15-US gallon) tank holds enough fuel to power the Aquada for around **90 minutes** on water.*

WaterCar Python This stylish high-speed prototype can reach speeds of more than 60 mph (96 km/h) as it skims over water.

Terrawind This 12.95-m- (42.5-ft-) long amphibious coach becomes a houseboat on water, with a kitchen, living area, and beds.

Room for one driver and two passengers

V6 engine under the bonnet gives vehicle power

AQU4DA

WOW!

In 2004, an Aquada driven by Sir Richard Branson smashed the record for an amphibious car crossing the **English Channel** by more than four hours, taking one hour, 40 minutes.

HOW TO FOLD-UP WHEELS

1. Sensors tell the car it is floating in water and must raise its wheels.

2. The wheels lift and tuck away into sealed spaces called housings. The power is cut from the engine to the wheels.

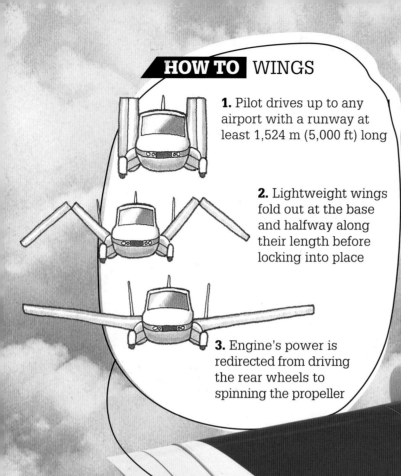

1. Pilot drives up to any airport with a runway at least 1,524 m (5,000 ft) long

2. Lightweight wings fold out at the base and halfway along their length before locking into place

3. Engine's power is redirected from driving the rear wheels to spinning the propeller

Wingspan of 8 m (26.5 ft)

IN THE AIR

The prototype of the Transition is making a test flight. Powered by a pusher propeller behind the plane's cockpit, it can cruise at a speed of 105 mph (172 km/h) and can travel up to 787 km (490 miles) in a single flight.

Cockpit built with a rigid safety cage made of carbon fibre

Flying high

When is a car not a car? When it turns into an aircraft, of course! Check out the fantastic feat of engineering that is the Terrafugia Transition. This plane can fold up its wings on the ground in less than 30 seconds. Then, it can drive along roads at speeds up to 65 mph (105 km/h) carrying a driver, passenger, and bags. No need for a taxi from the airport!

ON THE ROAD

With its wings tucked up, the Transition is 6 m (236 in) long, 2.3 m (90 in) wide, and can be driven on roads with the engine powering its rear wheels. It even has airbags for the driver and passenger.

Strong electromagnets lock the parts of the wing together for flying

10 On the **ground**, the Transition can be driven on any road and parked in a standard parking space.

30 The Transition can drive into any **petrol station** as it uses super-unleaded fuel.

20 You will need a **pilot's licence** with at least 20 hours of flight time to fly the Transition.

40 A pilot **flying** the Transition can use around 19 litres (5 US gallons) of fuel per hour in the air.

WOW!

If you want your own Terrafugia Transition (due to release late 2012), you better start saving now. The price for the basic aircraft is expected to be **US$279,000**.

N303TF

Twin tailfins help keep the aircraft stable as it flies

ENGINE POWER
100 hp Rotax 912S engine

SPEED
Air: 115 mph (185 km/h); land: 65 mph (105 km/h)

WEIGHT
653 kg (1,440 lb)

ORIGIN
USA

PAST AND FUTURE

Built by Moulton Taylor in 1956, this **Aerocar** flew until 1977. It was mainly used to fly and report on road traffic jams.

Powered by four fanlike engines, the **Moller Skycar M400** is being designed to take off and land vertically.

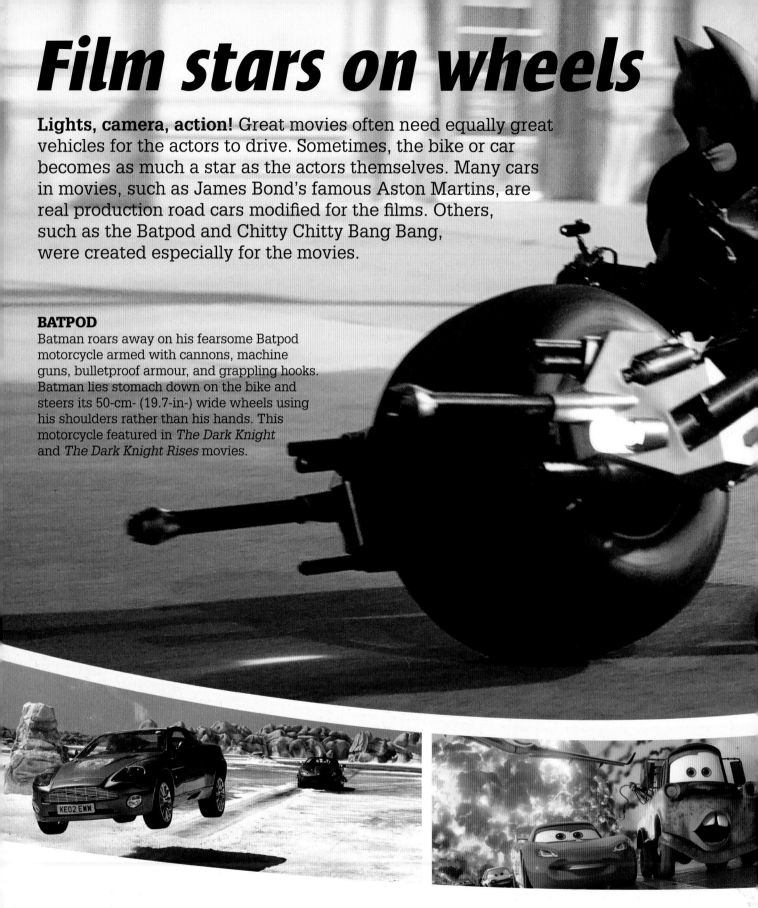

Film stars on wheels

Lights, camera, action! Great movies often need equally great vehicles for the actors to drive. Sometimes, the bike or car becomes as much a star as the actors themselves. Many cars in movies, such as James Bond's famous Aston Martins, are real production road cars modified for the films. Others, such as the Batpod and Chitty Chitty Bang Bang, were created especially for the movies.

BATPOD
Batman roars away on his fearsome Batpod motorcycle armed with cannons, machine guns, bulletproof armour, and grappling hooks. Batman lies stomach down on the bike and steers its 50-cm- (19.7-in-) wide wheels using his shoulders rather than his hands. This motorcycle featured in *The Dark Knight* and *The Dark Knight Rises* movies.

SUPER SPY CAR
Secret agent James Bond makes a spectacular escape in his Aston Martin V12 Vanquish in the movie *Die Another Day*. Bond's car is equipped with shotguns and five heat-seeking missiles.

ANIMATED WHEELS
The smash-hit animated movie *Cars 2* features a NASCAR-like racing car called Lightning McQueen (left) and his best friend, a tow truck called Mater (centre), in adventures in Japan, Italy, and England.

MY STORY: LINCOLN FUTURA

DATE BUILT 1955
ORIGINAL COST US$250,000
LENGTH 5.5 m (220 in)
STARRING ROLE 120 episodes of the *Batman* TV series

This futuristic concept car was designed by Ghia, Italy, for Ford's Lincoln division. It was sold to the famous car customizer George Barris for just US$1. He turned the car into the sleek and super-fast Batmobile, fitted with a smoke screen, battering ram, and the Bat-phone, for the 1960s *Batman* TV series.

TIME MACHINE

The movie *Back to the Future* featured a DeLorean DMC-12 sports car that could travel back in time when driving at 88 mph (142 km/h). In real life, some 9,000 DeLoreans were built, three of which had their body panels plated with gold and none of which could time travel.

UP, UP, AND AWAY

The author of the James Bond books, Ian Fleming, also wrote *Chitty Chitty Bang Bang* – the children's story about an old racing car that inventor Caractacus Potts turns into a flying vehicle. The story has been turned into a musical and a film, where the car was powered by a Ford 3000 V6 engine.

A giant truck speeds along an open highway hauling a crucial heavy load between distant towns. Many people work on the road using giant trucks, breakdown pickups, fire engines, and other emergency vehicles. Every day, vehicles help carry us from place to place. There is a range of vehicles that help us do what we need to do, from the most popular city car to one motor vehicle that is well and truly out of this world.

Live to drive

The red truck

Moving swiftly through traffic, sirens blaring, and lights flashing, fire trucks get to an emergency scene as quickly as possible. They are often the first vehicles to reach an emergency whether it is a fire, flood, road accident, or landslide. Even a handful of seconds saved can mean the difference between life and death.

WOW!
In the USA, Phoenix, Arizona's Hall of Flame is the **world's biggest** fire truck museum with more than 90 different fire engines.

PIERCE ENFORCER 2005
This large American fire engine contains lockers full of fire-fighting equipment as well as ladders, water tanks, and a powerful pump that can blast 5,678 litres (1,500 US gallons) of water every minute.

Sets of hoses can be pulled out of the truck to spray water or chemicals to put out a fire

HOW TO HYDRAULICS

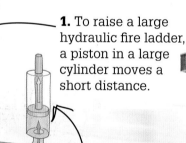

1. To raise a large hydraulic fire ladder, a piston in a large cylinder moves a short distance.

2. This pushes hydraulic liquid along a tube to smaller cylinders on the ladder.

3. The liquid pushes the pistons in the ladder a longer distance, extending the ladder.

ENGINE POWER
375–400 hp

SPEED
Around 70 mph
(113 km/h)

WEIGHT
Around 15,000 kg
(33,069 lb)

ORIGIN
USA

FIGHTING THE FLAMES

This **1927 Ford TT fire engine** carries a wooden ladder, a small water pump, and has a large searchlight on the front.

This **Carmichael Cobra 2** is an airport fire engine. It has five crew and up to 14,000 litres (3,698 US gallons) of water.

Bright lights flash to warn other traffic ahead

Diesel engine is tested and tuned regularly – the truck needs to work perfectly

Battering ram bumper can push items out of the way

FIRE DEPT.

Pierce

POLICE CARS

The police are out and about, cruising in patrol cars on the lookout for trouble and criminals. Some police cars are designed to be long-serving patrol cars or unmarked undercover vehicles. Others are flashier and faster – used for high-speed chases and to rush to emergency scenes. Here are eight great police cars, many of which are in service in more than one country.

CHEVY BEL AIR

ORIGIN USA
BUILT 1950–1975
IN SERVICE IN USA (to 1975) and Canada (to 1981)

HOLDEN COMMODORE

ORIGIN Australia
BUILT 1978
IN SERVICE IN Australia and New Zealand

LAMBORGHINI GALLARDO LP560-4

ORIGIN Italy
BUILT 2003
IN SERVICE IN Italy, South Korea, and UK

FORD CROWN VICTORIA POLICE INTERCEPTOR

ORIGIN USA
BUILT 1992–2011
IN SERVICE IN Canada and USA

THAT'S AMAZING!

The French police are known for driving cars that were made in their country. The Peugeot 307 is the car of choice used by the French police, but it is also a popular family car in many countries.

SKODA OCTAVIA
ORIGIN Czech Republic
BUILT 1996
IN SERVICE IN Czech Republic, Greece, and Poland

PORSCHE 911 CARRERA S
ORIGIN Germany
BUILT 2005, specially designed for fast policework
IN SERVICE IN Germany

HYUNDAI SONATA
ORIGIN Korea
BUILT 2001–2005
IN SERVICE IN China, Korea, Puerto Rico

SMART CAR
ORIGIN Germany
BUILT 1998
IN SERVICE IN Canada, Czech Republic, Italy, UK, and USA

Police motorbikes

Zipping and zigzagging through the traffic, thousands of motorbikes are used by the world's police forces. They perform many jobs, from helping the traffic run smoothly and escorting other vehicles, to patrolling neighbourhoods, racing to accidents, and catching criminals. Police motorcycles are often custom designed and fitted with special equipment, including sirens operated from the handlebars, extra lights, and tools stored in top boxes.

BE PREPARED

A Northern Ireland police officer speeds along on his BMW R1200RT-P motorcycle. This powerful bike is well packed with a siren, radios, extra lights, panniers at the back to store kit, and a second battery.

Extendable pole features bright, flashing LED lights at the top

Hard plastic panniers can hold police equipment

FAST FACTS

10 *The BMW R1200RT has a* **six speed gearbox**. *It can cover 402 m (quarter mile) from standing still in just 12 seconds.*

20 *Police officers have used motorbikes for* **traffic patrols** *and as* **escort vehicles** *since the early 20th century.*

30 *Motorbikes can* **speed up fast** *and can* **stop quickly** *if a police officer needs to dismount and run.*

40 *Some police forces use small* **scooters** *in busy city centres. Others use off-road bikes to reach isolated country places.*

FIRST AID AND FIRE

This **paramedic** motorbike has large panniers to store medical supplies used to treat accident and emergency victims.

A **fireman** performs a training exercise on a BMW R1200, specially kitted out with fire hoses and extinguishers.

ENGINE POWER
110 hp

SPEED
More than 124 mph (200 km/h)

WEIGHT
259 kg (571 lb)

ORIGIN
Germany

Shaped frame with windshield protects rider at high speed

HOW TO GLOBAL POSITIONING SYSTEM

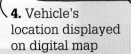

1. GPS satellites orbit Earth sending radio signals back to Earth

2. Satellite navigation device on motorbike receives signals from satellites

4. Vehicle's location displayed on digital map

3. Sat nav calculates distance from each satellite to pinpoint its own location

WOW!
In 2011, more than **80,000 BMW** motorcycles were in official use by police forces and emergency services in more than 150 countries.

Motorbikes in Asia

Beep, beep! The sound of horns fills the air. Motorbikes are popular all over the world, but in the busy roads of Asia, they are more than just a handy way to travel. They prove a lifeline to families who cannot afford to own a car or truck. Motorbikes are far cheaper to buy and repair than cars. They take up less room and smaller motorbikes use much less petrol than cars.

MY STORY:
SUPER CUB

ORIGIN Japan
MANUFACTURER Honda
FIRST BUILT 1958
ENGINE SIZE 49 cc
TANK 4 litres (1.1 US gallons)

This simple, reliable motorbike is the world's most popular. It uses less than 0.7 litre (0.18 US gallons) of fuel to drive 100 km (62 miles), which makes it cheap to run. In 2008, the 60 millionth Super Cub was sold, making it the best-selling motor vehicle in history.

BUSY STREET

This traffic jam in the centre of the city of Hanoi in Vietnam is crammed full of motorbikes, with only the occasional cyclist and pedestrian. Apart from being cheaper to run, motorcycles can weave in and out of crowded city streets, zipping past other vehicles easily.

HUGE LOAD

A couple with a massive load of rugs and cloth travel by motorbike through Cambodia's capital city, Phnom Penh. More than half of the world's motorbikes are found in Asian countries such as Cambodia.

FIVE ON BOARD

Do not try this at home! A family of five ride a motorcycle in Bali, Indonesia. Small motorbikes overloaded with whole families going to school and work are a common sight in many countries in Asia.

TUK-TUK

Popular in Sri Lanka, Thailand, and other Asian nations, tuk-tuks are named after the sound the engine makes when it runs. These three wheeled machines use a motorbike engine, but have a covered cabin for passengers.

3. The cable winds slowly, but with great force, pulling the broken-down vehicle.

1. A winch's strong metal cable rolls onto a cylinder called a drum.

2. The turning speed is reduced and the turning force increased by gear cogs.

HOWARD SOMMERS TOWING, INC.

7891 DEERING AVE.
CANOGA PARK, CA.

(818) 884-5600

Breakdown!

Pffft... splutter... stop. Millions of cars, trucks, and motorbikes stop running and working every year. Tough, reliable, and strong breakdown trucks tow these stricken vehicles out of danger to nearby garages for repair. Apart from winches and powerful lifting arms called booms, tow trucks may also carry a wide range of tools, from metal cutters to spanners and crowbars.

WOW!
The Royal Automobile Club (RAC) is one breakdown service in the UK. In 2010, its vehicles went to attend more than **2.5 million** breakdowns.

ENGINE POWER	SPEED	WEIGHT	ORIGIN

600 hp	26 mph (42 km/h)	33,565 kg (74,000 lb)	USA

Large diesel engine must generate enough power to drive both the truck and the vehicle it tows

FAST FACTS

10 *Mechanic Ernest Holmes built the **first breakdown truck** in 1916 in Chattanooga, USA.*

20 *Many tow trucks have a heavy **counterweight** fitted near the front to stop the truck tipping up when lifting.*

30 *A **Caterpillar truck** (see page 63) works as a tow vehicle. It weighs more than 200 tonnes (221 US tons).*

KENWORTH C500
This breakdown truck backs into place. It uses its powerful winch mechanism to pull a vehicle out of a ditch. The long arm, called a boom, helps lift vehicles up and out of trouble.

TO THE RESCUE

A British **breakdown service van** attends to a broken down car. Many engine faults can be fixed by the roadside.

Cars, like this BMW, which cannot be easily fixed or towed may be lifted away from the road by truck with a **crane**.

A broken-down car may be carried on a **flatbed transporter truck** to a garage or wrecker's yard.

TRY THIS FOR SIZE

Meet the heavy haulers. Articulated or "artic" trucks are two-part vehicles. The front part consists of the engine and the driver's cab. It is connected to a wheeled trailer by a joint called the fifth wheel. This joint can swivel, allowing the truck to go around tight corners. It also means that different types of trailer can be hitched and driven by the cab.

SCANIA R 730

Designed for long-distance hauling, this truck's fuel tank holds 300 litres (79 US gallons). Extra fuel tanks can be added. When fully loaded, the truck and its trailer can weigh up to 60,000 kg (132,277 lb).

LOADED UP

Many artics haul **giant tanks** full of liquid fuels, such as petrol, chemicals, or even refrigerated milk.

A **Peterbilt 388 truck** transports three other Peterbilt trucks across the outback of Australia.

HOW TO FIFTH WHEEL

1. Fifth wheel is covered in grease to reduce friction

2. Metal post on the trailer, called the king pin, slots into the fifth wheel

3. Trailer swings from side to side behind the cab when turning

WOW!

In 2006, a Mack truck pulled a record **112 trailers** a distance of 100 m (328 ft). The truck and trailers measured 1.47 km (0.9 miles) long!

ENGINE POWER
730 hp

SPEED
92 mph
(148 km/h)

WEIGHT
Approx 8,500 kg
(18,739 lb)

ORIGIN
Sweden

FAST FACTS

10 The *first artic* was made in the 1910s. A tractor-like truck pulled a wagon that was normally driven by horses.

20 The R730 artic has *14 gears* for all conditions, from cruising open roads to climbing a steep hill.

30 At the Granites Gold Mine in Australia, one truck hauls *six trailers* at the same time.

TOPLINE

SCANIA

R 730

SZK 910

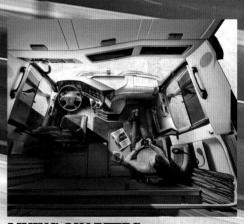

LIVING QUARTERS
A long-distance truck driver often has to live in a cab for days at a time. The interior of the Scania R 730 includes a fold-down full-sized bed, a pull-out table, and a coffee maker.

Truck engine cooled by air entering through these grilles

ICE ROAD TRUCKERS

Wrap up warm and join the fearless ice road truckers deep inside the Arctic Circle. Here, small communities live and work in the coldest of conditions. In the past, only dog sleds could travel across areas where real roads could not be found. Today, crucial transport links are provided by ice roads made in winter over frozen rivers and lakes. The truckers haul their heavy loads along these temporary and sometimes perilous tracks.

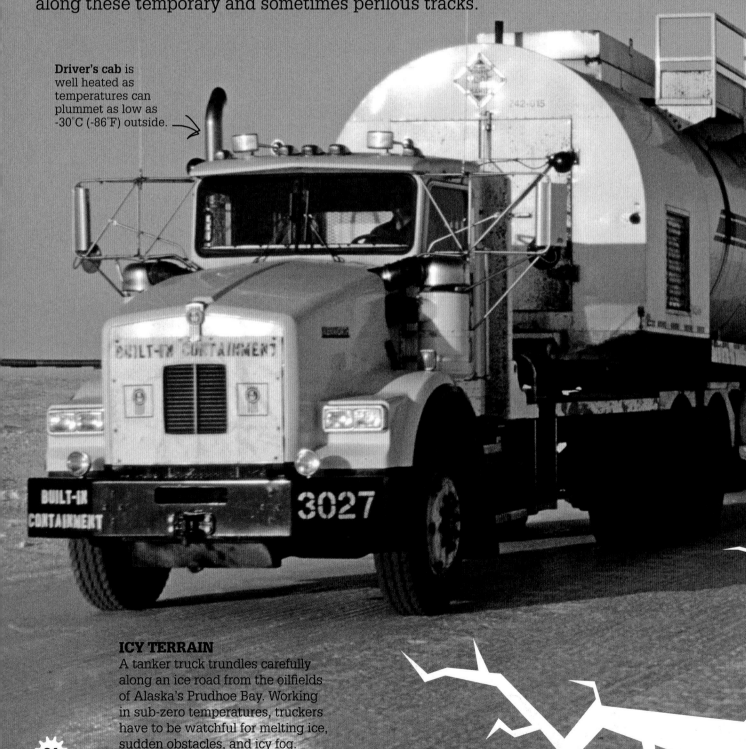

Driver's cab is well heated as temperatures can plummet as low as -30°C (-86°F) outside. →

ICY TERRAIN
A tanker truck trundles carefully along an ice road from the oilfields of Alaska's Prudhoe Bay. Working in sub-zero temperatures, truckers have to be watchful for melting ice, sudden obstacles, and icy fog.

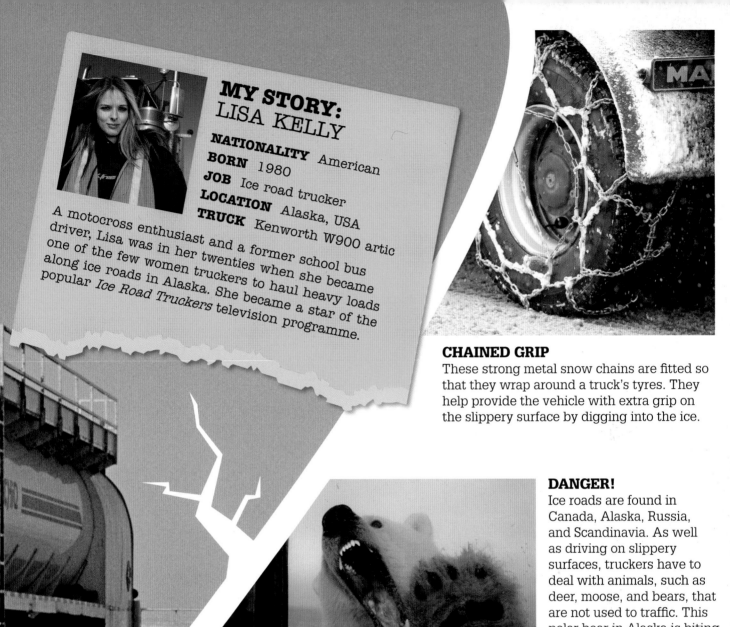

MY STORY:
LISA KELLY

NATIONALITY American
BORN 1980
JOB Ice road trucker
LOCATION Alaska, USA
TRUCK Kenworth W900 artic

A motocross enthusiast and a former school bus driver, Lisa was in her twenties when she became one of the few women truckers to haul heavy loads along ice roads in Alaska. She became a star of the popular *Ice Road Truckers* television programme.

CHAINED GRIP

These strong metal snow chains are fitted so that they wrap around a truck's tyres. They help provide the vehicle with extra grip on the slippery surface by digging into the ice.

DANGER!

Ice roads are found in Canada, Alaska, Russia, and Scandinavia. As well as driving on slippery surfaces, truckers have to deal with animals, such as deer, moose, and bears, that are not used to traffic. This polar bear in Alaska is biting a window of a stationary truck, but no one was hurt.

CRACKING UP

Truckers, such as this one in Canada, must watch out for melting or cracking ice and follow weight and speed limits for their vehicles. If a truck weighs more than the limit, it can sink through thin ice. The freezing temperatures can cause frostbite or even death for a driver stranded without a heated cab in which to wait for rescue.

TOYOTA PRIUS

In 1997, the Toyota Prius became the first mass-produced hybrid vehicle. This sleek 2009 model uses its petrol engine for fast driving, but the electric motor to help pull away at low speeds.

Door sensor senses driver holding key approaching and unlocks doors automatically

Fuel savers

Imagine having two engines! Hybrid cars have a regular engine, fuelled by petrol, but they also contain one or more motors powered by electricity. Amazingly, two motors can be better than one with the electric motor helping out the petrol engine at times. This leads to the petrol engine using less fuel and a more fuel-efficient car.

WOW!
Good fuel efficiency means that the Prius can travel up to **1,152 km** (716 miles) on one tank of petrol! That's London to Paris and back, with half a fuel tank left over!

FAST FACTS

10 When **going uphill**, the electric motor cuts in to reduce the fuel used by the petrol engine.

20 When **slowing down**, the energy of movement is recycled to help recharge the electric motor battery.

30 In **Electric Vehicle (EV) mode**, the Prius can be driven short distances on the electric motor alone.

40 On warm days, **solar panels** on the sunroof power an electric fan to keep the car cool.

ENGINE POWER
134 hp combined power

SPEED
112 mph (180 km/h)

WEIGHT
1,379 kg (3,040 lb)

ORIGIN
Japan

HOW TO ELECTRIC MOTOR

1. Rechargeable battery powers the electric motor

2. Energy from wheels braking turns the generator

3. Generator makes electricity that recharges the battery

4. Electric motor turns the wheels to start the car moving

TWO ENGINES ARE BETTER THAN ONE

The groovy **Piaggio MP3** hybrid motorcycle can travel up to 60 km (37 miles) on a single litre (0.26 US gallon) of petrol.

The **Ford Escape** is a 4.4-m- (174-in-) long hybrid SUV. It can travel up to 800 km (497 miles) on a single tank of petrol.

This sporty looking **Honda CR-Z** coupé is a hybrid that was launched in 2010. It has a top speed of 124 mph (199.5 km/h).

Green machines

Petrol vehicles may soon be overtaken by those using alternative energy. Petrol and diesel are fuels that come from oil. Our planet has only limited supplies of oil, and burning it in engines causes air pollution. So these amazing vehicles, from historic times to the future, are powered by alternative sources – electricity stored in batteries, chemical reactions in fuel cells, wind, or the energy from sunlight.

LOHNER PORSCHE

ORIGIN Germany
DATE 1899
POWER Hybrid
TOP SPEED 37 mph (60 km/h)

TESLA ROADSTER

ORIGIN USA
DATE 2009
POWER Electric batteries
TOP SPEED 125 mph (201 km/h)

MITSUBISHI I MIEV

ORIGIN Japan
DATE 2009
POWER Electric batteries
TOP SPEED 81 mph (130 km/h)

NISSAN LEAF

ORIGIN Japan
DATE 2010
POWER Electric batteries
TOP SPEED 93 mph (150 km/h)

THAT'S AMAZING!

There are both hybrid and electric versions of the tiny Smart Fortwo city car. During a promotional campaign to celebrate the Smart's tenth anniversary, 13 gymnasts managed to squeeze inside this two-seater micro car.

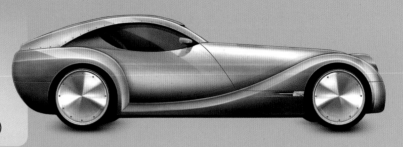

MORGAN LIFECAR

ORIGIN UK
DATE 2006–2008
POWER Hydrogen fuel cell
TOP SPEED 79 mph (150 km/h)

AURORA 101

ORIGIN Australia
DATE 2006
POWER Solar panels driving electric motor
TOP SPEED 94.5 mph (152 km/h)

NLV QUANT (CONCEPT)

ORIGIN Switzerland/Sweden
DATE 2010–2011
POWER Solar with electric battery
TOP SPEED 234 mph (377 km/h)

GREENBIRD

ORIGIN UK
DATE 2006–2008
POWER Wind power
TOP SPEED 125 mph (203 km/h)

MOON MOTORS
NASA astronaut Eugene Cernan drives the Apollo 17 rover shortly after arriving on the Moon. The rover's two 36-volt batteries provided power for the four electric motors, one for each wheel.

T-handle in the middle of the rover allows astronaut to steer and go forward or reverse

Carrier at the back holds hand tools for use by the astronauts on the Moon's surface

Wheels are 22.9 cm (9 in) wide and made of steel strands with a titanium tread

LUNAR ROVER

WOW!
The three lunar rovers that made it to the Moon **remain there** today. For each minute they were driven on the lunar surface, they cost more than US$58,000!

Here's a car that is out of this world! In 1971, astronauts drove the first ever vehicle on the Moon. The Lunar Roving Vehicle was ferried up in the Apollo 15 spacecraft, tightly packed away for storage. After touchdown, the rover was rolled out and driven away, giving astronauts wheels to explore more of the Moon's surface. Four rovers were built and three made it to the Moon, each able to carry two astronauts, cameras, and equipment.

HOW TO UNPACK THE ROVER

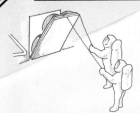

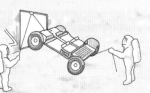

1. Apollo craft's side panel becomes ramp as cable is pulled down

2. Rear part of rover unfolds and locks into position

3. Front part of rover locks as it is lowered to the Moon's surface

4. Cable is disconnected and seats are unfolded – rover is unpacked!

TEST-DRIVEN

The **Apollo 16 rover** is test driven over a model of the Moon's surface at the Kennedy Space Centre in Florida, USA.

This **future rover** being driven on Earth runs on 12 wheels. It can house astronauts for missions lasting up to 14 days.

ENGINE POWER
1 hp

SPEED
8 mph
(13 km/h)

WEIGHT
209 kg
(460 lb)

ORIGIN
USA

FAST FACTS

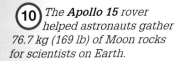

10 The **Apollo 15** rover helped astronauts gather 76.7 kg (169 lb) of Moon rocks for scientists on Earth.

20 The rover could cross **crevasses** (gaps) up to 70 cm (28 in) wide and drive on slopes up to 25 degrees.

30 The **Apollo 17** rover travelled the furthest, completing 35.9 km (22 miles) of exploration.

40 Laminated maps and tape were used to **repair** a bumper when the Apollo 17 rover became damaged.

Glossary

acceleration
To speed up and go faster.

aluminium
A metal that is light in weight and is used for some car parts.

battery
A store of chemicals in a case that when connected to a circuit supplies electricity.

brake discs
A type of brake where pads press against a turning disc to create friction and slow the wheel down.

bumper
A metal, rubber, or plastic bar fitted along the front and back of a vehicle to limit damage to a car or truck if it bumps into something.

carbon fibre
An advanced material made to be light in weight but very strong.

cargo bed
The area behind a truck's cab where objects, known as freight or cargo, can be carried.

cc
Short for cubic capacity, this measurement is how much space there is inside all the cylinders of an engine. A larger cc usually means a more powerful engine.

chauffeur
A person employed to drive a vehicle to transport a person from place to place.

concept vehicle
A vehicle that is built not to be sold, but to demonstrate new designs or technologies.

coupé
A two-door car that seats two to four people.

customize
To change a vehicle's design, body, and other parts so that it looks very different.

diesel
A type of fuel, made from oil, that is used in many truck and some car engines.

differential
A part of a car or truck that splits the engine power to each wheel so wheels can turn at different speeds when going around corners.

downforce
A force created by a car travelling through the air that presses down on the car, helping to increase the tyre's grip of the road or track.

exhaust
Tubes that channel waste gases away from a vehicle's engine and out into the open air.

forks
A part of a motorbike that connects the front wheel and axle to the frame.

Formula One (F1)
A worldwide motor racing championship featuring very fast single-seater cars.

four-wheel drive
A system in a vehicle where power from the engine is sent to turn all four wheels.

friction
The force that slows movement between two objects that rub together. Brakes create a lot of friction to slow a car down.

fuel
A substance or material that is burned to produce heat or power. In most vehicles, petrol or diesel is used as a fuel.

fuel cell
A device that creates power by converting energy from chemical reactions (such as hydrogen reacting with oxygen) into electricity.

gears
Toothed wheels that are used to change the speed or force with which car wheels turn.

generator
A machine that creates electricity for use by electric motors or lights.

Grand Prix
An important car or motorcycle race. Formula One races are all called Grand Prix.

hatchback
A small car with a rear door and window covering the boot area.

horsepower (hp)
A unit of power used to measure the power of a motor vehicle engine.

hybrid vehicle
A vehicle that has both a petrol engine and another engine or motor such as an electric motor.

hydraulics
A system that uses the pushing force of liquid and cylinders inside tubes to create movement.

layshaft
A rod that has toothed wheel gears built into it as part of a vehicle's gear system.

LED
Short for light emitting diode, an LED is a small but very bright light.

lithium battery
A type of battery using the element lithium that can be recharged after it has run out. It can be used to power a vehicle.

motocross
A type of motorcycle sport where riders race around laps of a cross-country course filled with bumps, dips, and jumps.

MotoGP
Short for Motorcycle Grand Prix racing, MotoGP is a competition held every year with a series of races held on circuits for leading riders.

NASCAR
NASCAR (National Association for Stock Car Auto Racing) is a popular type of car racing in North America featuring powerful saloons.

off-road
To travel in a vehicle away from roads and over tracks, trails, or open ground.

panniers
Boxes or bags attached to a bike for storage.

petrol
A liquid fuel, made from oil, that is burned inside most vehicle engines.

piston
A rod-shaped engine part that moves up and down inside an engine cylinder.

pit stop
A break in which a racing vehicle leaves the racetrack for repairs and tyre changes.

radiator
A part of a vehicle that uses water or another liquid to help cool down the engine.

road train
An articulated truck that pulls two or more trailers.

saloon
A four-door family car with an enclosed boot area.

solar panel
A device that converts energy from sunlight into electricity.

streamlined
To be shaped so that air flows easily over and around it.

supercar
An expensive, fast, high-performance car.

suspension
A system of springs and shock absorbers that helps make a vehicle travel smoothly over bumps and dips.

swingarm
A movable joint between the rear wheel and the body of a motorcycle.

tank
A container that holds fuel, such as petrol or diesel, for the engine.

throttle
A device for controlling the speed of the engine and the vehicle.

thrust
A force that propels a vehicle forward.

turbine
A machine, often shaped like a wheel, with blades that are turned by a liquid or gas.

valve
An opening in an engine cylinder that opens and closes to let fuel and air in or gases out.

Index

Credits

DK would like to thank:
Ashwin Khurana and James Mitchem for additional editorial work, and Mary Sandberg for additional design. Clare Gray for proofreading. Jackie Brind for preparing the index.

DK India would like to thank:
Sudakshina Basu for design assistance.

All illustrations by Daniel Wright.

The publisher would like to thank the following for their kind permission to reproduce their photographs:

Key: a – above; b – below; c – centre; f – far; l – left; t – top

4 SuperStock: Transtock. **5 Corbis:** David Madison (t). **SuperStock:** Flirt (b). **6 Ford Motor Company Limited:** europeanmotornews.com (cl). **Chrysler and Jeep Marketing:** (c). **Harley-Davidson Motor Company:** (bc). **KTM-Sportmotorcycle AG:** (br). **Scania CV AB (publ):** Göran Wink (cr). **7 Alamy Images:** Nick Baylis (clb). **BMW AG:** (bl). **Ford Motor Company Limited:** (ca). **Chrysler and Jeep Marketing:** (tr). **Corbis:** Bettmann (tl). **Dreamstime.com:** Robwilson3... (cb). **Volvo Car UK Ltd:** (cl). **8–9 Corbis:** David Madison. **10–11 Chris Walker (Kartpix.net).** **10 Rex Features:** Action Press (l). **11 Alamy Images:** Joe Fox Motorsport (tc). **Birel S.P.A.:** (tl). **12 Corbis:** DPA (t). **12–13 Getty Images.** **13 Corbis:** EPA (bl). **Getty Images:** (br, bc). **14 Corbis:** Jean-Yves Ruszniewski/TempSport (bl). **Dorling Kindersley:** (ca, cb); James Mann (t). **15 Dorling Kindersley:** (c). **Mark Haverty:** Flickr (ca). **16–17 Toyota Motorsport:** Lesley Ann Miller LAT Photo USA (t). **17 Getty Images:** (br). **Toyota Motorsport:** Lesley Ann Miller LAT Photo USA (bc). **18–19 Getty Images:** (t). **18 Getty Images:** (b). **19 Getty Images:** (t, bl, r). **20–21 Corbis:** Chris Williams/Icon SMI. **20 Corbis:** Walter G. Arce/Cal Sport Media/Zuma Press (t). **21 Alamy Images:** Kelvin Webb (tl). **Corbis:** David Griffin/Icon SMI (tr). **22–23 Getty Images.** **23 Victory and Victory Motorcycles® are registered trademarks of Polaris Industries Inc:** (tr). **Vintage Superbikes/Brian O'Shea:** (tl). **24 Getty Images:** (tl). **Press Association Images:** AP Photo/Petros Giannakouris (tr). **TopFoto.co.uk:** National Motor Museum/HIP (c). **24–25 Getty Images:** AFP (b). **25 Murray Turner:** (tl). **26–27 Yamaha Motor.** **27 Apache Quads:** Dan Le Marchant from Guernsey on his Apache SX 100 SilverSport (cr). **Getty Images:** (tl); MCT (tr).

28 Kawasaki (UK): (tr). **KTM-Sportmotorcycle AG:** (br). **Zdenek Zenyt:** Flickr (bl). **30–31 Alamy Images:** Richard McDowell (t). **31 Alamy Images:** imagebroker (br). **Harold Hinson:** (bl). **32–33 Press Association Images:** AP/Natacha Pisarenko. **32 Getty Images:** (b). **33 Amaury Sport Organisation:** (cr, br). **Corbis:** Yves Forestier/Sygma (t). **34–35 Robert Haught, AllMonster. com.** **35 Alamy Images:** F1online digitale Bildagentur GmbH (cr). **BigFoot 4x4, Inc.:** www.Bigfoot4x4.com (tr). **Corbis:** Duomo (tl). **36–37 Corbis:** EPA (t). **36 Alamy Images:** Thomas Frey / imagebroker (br). **Press Association Images:** Peter Cosgrove (bl). **37 Corbis:** Frank Hoppen/Transtock (br); Imaginechina (bl); Michael Ochs Archives (ca). **38–39 Harley-Davidson Motor Company.** **39 Alamy Images:** Simon Clay (tl). **Getty Images:** (b). **Harley-Davidson Motor Company:** (tr). **40–41 Alamy Images:** Transtock Inc. **41 Alamy Images:** culture-images GmbH (tr). **Corbis:** Transtock Inc. (cr). **43 Corbis:** Imaginechina (ca). **2008 SSC, Inc/www.shelbysupercars.com:** (cb). **44–45 Getty Images:** (c). **44 Bloodhound SSC/Curventa and Siemens:** (bl). **45 Mike Akatiff:** (ca). **JCB:** (t). **Mark Nearburg:** (br). **46–47 SuperStock:** Transtock. **48–49 Alamy Images:** Tom Wood. **48 Corbis:** (bl). **49 Alamy Images:** Stan Rohrer (tl). **Getty Images:** Car Culture (tc). **50 Bertone, Caprie (TO) Italy:** (b). **Corbis:** Bettmann (clb); (tl, c). **51 Corbis:** Car Culture (b). **Keio University, Electric Vehicle Laboratory:** (c). **Mercedes-Benz Cars, Daimler AG:** (cra). **Nissan Motor Company:** (cb). **52–53 Corbis:** Transtock Inc. **52 Getty Images:** Hulton Archive (bl). **Nick Williams:** (br). **53 Autostadt GmbH, Wolfsburg, Germany:** Chris Franjkovic (br). **Photoshot:** Michael Hanschke (bl). **54 Corbis:** Jana Renee Cruder (cr); Transtock Inc.: (tl). **Getty Images:** Car Culture (cl). **SuperStock:** imagebroker.net (tr). **55 Alamy Images:** Mark Scheuern (cr). **Corbis:** Car Culture (tl, cl). **SuperStock:** imagebroker.net (tr). **56–57 Jon Muresan.** **57 Honda (UK):** (tl). **Suzuki Motor Corporation:** (tc). **Victory and Victory Motorcycles® are registered trademarks of Polaris Industries Inc.:** (tr). **58 Alamy Images:** Michael Booth (bc); Peter Jordan_NE: (br). **58–59 BMW AG.** **59 Alamy Images:** Peter E. Noyce (tr). **60 Corbis:** Bettmann (cr); Transtock Inc.: (cl).

Louwman Museum-The Hague: (tl). **Magic Car Pics:** (tr). **61 Mercedes-Benz Cars, Daimler AG:** (tl). **62 Alamy Images:** James Cheadle (b). **Getty Images:** (c). **Ultimatecarpage.com/Wouter Melissen:** (t). **63 Corbis:** Transtock Inc.: (t). **Getty Images:** MCT (b). **66–67 Terrafugia, Inc.:** (c). **66 Dan Dawson Photography:** (b). **67 Alamy Images:** I. Glory (br). **Press Association Images:** AP Photo (bl). **68–69 Rex Features:** Warner Bros/Everett. **68 Rex Features:** Everett/BuenaVist (br). **The Ronald Grant Archive:** (bl). **69 Corbis:** Noah Dodson/Retna Ltd. (bc). **Getty Images:** (t). **The Kobal Collection:** Warfield/United Artists (cr). **70–71 SuperStock:** Flirt. **72–73 SuperStock:** Transtock (b). **73 Alamy Images:** Motoring Picture Library (tl); Sandy Young (tl). **74 Alamy Images:** Adam James (tl). **Ford Motor Company Limited:** (b). **Corbis:** Reuters (cb). **Andrew Scutter:** (c). **75 Alamy Images:** AA World Travel Library (cb); Ruslan Bustamante (t); vario images GmbH & Co. KG (b). **Porsche AG:** (c). **Škoda Auto a.s.:** (cra). **76–77 Alamy Images:** Joe Fox. **77 Alamy Images:** Shout (tl). **Reuters:** Phil Noble (tl). **78 Getty Images:** Bruno De Hogues. **Honda (UK):** (cl). **79 Getty Images:** AFP (t, b); Nicholas De Vore (cr). **80–81 Alamy Images:** Scott Tucker. **81 Alamy Images:** Justin Kase (br); Transportimage Picture Library (bl); Shout (bc). **82–83 Scania CV AB (publ):** Göran Wink. **82 Nick Borzo:** (cl, bl). **83 Daimler AG:** (tr). **84–85 SuperStock:** imagebroker. net. **85 Alamy Images:** Steven J. Kazlowski (c). **Corbis:** Fred de Noyelle (t). **Getty Images:** Richard Olsenius (b). **History Channel:** (tl). **86–87 Toyota Motor Europe.** **87 Alamy Images:** izmostock (bc). **Honda (UK):** (br). **Piaggio Veicoli Europei Spa:** (bl). **88 Alamy Images:** Drive Images (c). **Mitsubishi Motors Corporation:** (cb). **Nissan Motor Company:** Francesc Montero – www.fmimages.com (b). **Porsche AG:** (tl). **89 Alamy Images:** AlamyCelebrity (cb). **Corbis:** Reuters (c). **Greenbird (www.greenbird.co.uk):** Peter Lyons (b). **Morgan Motor Company Ltd:** (ca). **90–91 NASA. 91 NASA:** (tr, cr). **94–95 Dorling Kindersley:** Phil Townend.

Jacket images: *Front:* **Alamy Images:** Oleksiy Maksymenko. **Corbis:** Don Heiny bl; Chris Ryan br; Transtock bc. *Back:* **Alamy Images:** izmostock cb. **Corbis:** Car Culture clb. **Dorling Kindersley:** Geoff Mitchell crb.

All other images © Dorling Kindersley
For further information see:
www.dkimages.com